DECAL

T0246799

Van der Graaf Generator
in the 1970s

Steve Pilkington

SONIC**BOND**

sonicbondpublishing.com

Sonicbond Publishing Limited
www.sonicbondpublishing.co.uk
Email: info@sonicbondpublishing.co.uk

First Published in the United Kingdom 2022
First Published in the United States 2022

British Library Cataloguing in Publication Data:
A Catalogue record for this book is available from the British Library

ISBN 978-1-78952-245-7

Typeset in ITC Garamond & ITC Avant Garde
Printed and bound in England

Graphic design and typesetting: Full Moon Media

Acknowledgements

Firstly, I would like to thank all of the members of Van der Graaf Generator, past and present, for the remarkable body of work they have left us with. It remains unparallelled.

Particular thanks are due to Hugh Banton and Guy Evans, who have been very generous with their time in speaking to me for this book – their recollections have proven invaluable.

I would also like to give notable thanks to Peter Hammill, for having been a gracious and polite conversationalist in the past when I have had the pleasure of interviewing him – and also for the inspiration which his words in particular have provided me with over the years. To paraphrase Bob Dylan's decades-old quote about Smokey Robinson, I have long contended that 'Peter Hammill is England's Greatest Living Poet'.

I would also like to thank Stephen Lambe of Sonicbond Publishing, whose continued support of my writings has been a thing of gratefully accepted wonder over the years, and makes me think I must be doing something right...

Thanks as well to my wife Janet, who has patiently provided a listening post to this evolving document, firstly to assist in spotting any errors, but eventually being drawn into the strange saga of VdGG!

Acknowledgement is especially due to the expansive tome *Van Der Graaf Generator: The Book* by Phil Smart and Jim Christopulos, which is an invaluable work. Additional thanks are due to Phil for assistance with photographs, and both for their support and encouragement.

Finally, and as alluded to in the introduction to this story, this book is gratefully dedicated to the man whose name is lost to my imperfect memory yet who set me on my own personal VdGG journey over four decades ago. If you are reading this, a sincere and long-belated 'thank you'.

DECADES | Van der Graaf Generator in the 1970s

Contents

Introduction – Van der Graaf Generator: A Personal Journey

My own journey with Van der Graaf Generator began in a faltering way in early 1976 when, aged 14, I bought a copy of *Still Life* after reading a glowing review. I say 'faltering', because I sold it again almost immediately! My 14-year-old musical mind, while happy to absorb the likes of Zeppelin, Floyd, Sabbath and ELP, was woefully unprepared for its initiation into the VdGG circle, and for a few years, that seemed to be that.

Fast forward to 1981 and, aged 20, I was living in a Halls of Residence in London, attending the Central London Polytechnic. One night, I was in a gathering of people when a guy (whose name is lost to me over the mists of time) mentioned Peter Hammill. I remembered my brief encounter with *Still Life* and told him about it. 'Do you have a cassette player here?' he asked, and I replied that yes, indeed I did – as my vinyl albums and stereo system had been too bulky to transport from home. He immediately went and fetched a tape which had the *Still Life* album on it. 'Just do this for me,' he said. 'Take this and listen to it once each evening for ten days. Then give it back to me. If you still don't care for it, we'll never mention it again.'

Intrigued, I took it and dutifully listened to the album each evening. For the first two or three days, it still wasn't really grabbing me, but then, around day number four, things started coming together and making musical sense. From that point, as each day went by, more and more pieces of this incredible musical jigsaw moved themselves into place in my brain, and by the tenth day, I not only handed him the tape back but also showed him the vinyl copy I had gone out and bought that same day. It had me, and I was hooked. So much so that I went on to carry that forward, and over the subsequent years, I lent a copy of that album to anyone who I thought may be receptive to it, with those same 'ten days' instructions. The hit rate was very high.

Following that, I picked up a copy of the compilation *68–71* and got a taste of the earlier material. Once again, I wasn't sure at first, but this time it took only a couple of listens before I was sucked in. From there, I launched myself entirely and happily into fandom. I tracked down and devoured all of the band's albums, moving on then to everything Peter Hammill had released solo up to that point, and even a second-hand copy I was delighted to find of *The Long Hello*, the album recorded by the rest of the band without Hammill.

I even attended a poetry reading evening one night in those student days (there was free food, I was a student, that's how it was), and I got up and recited the lyrics to the song 'Still Life'. It is testament to the genius of Peter Hammill as a wordsmith that not only did it elicit enthusiastic applause, but not a single person in the room had any idea it was in fact a song lyric until I told them. Decades later, when I finally met and interviewed Peter himself, I told him that story, and was proud to do so.

It has often been said that the best music is that which takes time to reveal its full charms. That maxim is certainly true in the case of Van der Graaf Generator, as to this day, almost without exception, whenever I have heard an album for the first time I have initially thought, 'Hmm, no, not quite the top shelf stuff, this,' only for those metaphorical jigsaw pieces to arrange themselves in my mind once again and work their magic. It has also often been said that once you are hooked into the world of VdGG, you are in for good. Nothing could be truer. I will admit that, of course, as with every artist, not everything produced by VdGG or, indeed, Hammill solo has me believing it to be faultless. For example, I still reserve slightly less enthusiasm for the VdG (without the 'Generator') period of the late 1970s. However, taken as a whole, the material put out by Van der Graaf Generator and Peter Hammill over the course of the 1970s is as close to perfect as any band I could name. And *Still Life* is, to this day, still my favourite album of all time, by anyone.

As I said, I cannot remember the name of that unknown ambassador of Van der Graaf back in 1981 – but nonetheless, this book is dedicated to him with my eternal gratitude. If he is reading this, perhaps he will get in touch. Stranger things have happened in the world of Van der Graaf Generator – and a lot of them will be revealed in these pages.

Starting The Van – Pre-1970 Beginnings

The Aerosol Grey Machine

Personnel:
Peter Hammill: lead vocals, acoustic guitar
Hugh Banton: organ, piano, percussion, backing vocals
Keith Ellis: bass guitar
Guy Evans: drums
Additional personnel:
Jeff Peach: flute on 'Running Back'
Recorded at Marquee and Trident Studios, January, July and August 1969
Produced by John Anthony
Released: September 1969 (Initially US only, Mercury)
Highest chart places: Did not chart
Running time: 46:58
Tracklisting:
1. 'Afterwards' (Hammill) 4.55, 2. 'Orthentian Street' (Hammill) 6.18, 3. 'Running Back' (Hammill) 6.35, 4. 'Into A Game' (Hammill, Banton, Ellis, Evans) 6.57, 5. 'Aerosol Grey Machine' (Hammill) 0.47, 6. 'Black Smoke Yen' (Banton, Ellis, Evans) 1.26, 7. 'Aquarian' (Hammill) 8.22, 8. 'Necromancer' (Hammill) 3.30, 9. 'Octopus' (Hammill) 8.00

The story of Van der Graaf Generator is, undeniably and inextricably, bound up with that of Peter Hammill. Founder, vocalist, chief songwriter and – to most people at least – de facto bandleader, he is inevitably the focal point when the band gets discussed – although they were in fact run in the main on a very democratic basis.

Peter Joseph Andrew Hammill was born on 5 November 1948 in Ealing, Surrey, though he moved to Derby with his parents when he was 12 years old. After attending the prestigious Roman Catholic public school, Beaumont College (near to Eton, in Old Windsor), Hammill went to study the rather nebulous-sounding Liberal Studies in Science at Manchester University in 1967, and it is at this point where the Van der Graaf Generator story really starts. Soon after his arrival in Manchester, Hammill met Chris Judge Smith (Judge was his actual middle name – he has said that he liked to use the name Judge Smith as it got him better service in restaurants), a flamboyant and somewhat eccentric character who had recently returned from a trip across the USA which had fired his imagination and inspired him to, as he put it, 'write weird music'. An already arresting figure at a thin and gangly six feet-plus, he enhanced that appearance with his prematurely balding hairline, round owlish spectacles and a penchant for retro-styled three-piece suits and a pocket watch on a chain. Even among students in the late 1960s, that wasn't a regular look.

Living on a large campus residential site called, rather grandly, Fallowfield Student Village, people forming bands was a not uncommon occurrence, and it was here that the very first fledgling VdGG played their inaugural performance. A core trio of Hammill on guitar, Smith on drums and another student named Nick Pearne on guitar had already played a show of sorts, providing music for a poetry event called 'Outcome', and the trio formed the first rough incarnation of VdGG after responding to an advertisement for musicians placed by Colin Wilkinson, a harmonica player among other things. Pearne was normally a keyboard player, despite that earlier appearance. There were also, in one of the most incongruous pairings that could be imagined, two 'go-go dancers' named Keren and Maggie augmenting the band's show! They didn't last too long, in fairness, but one has to imagine that, when considering seemingly tall tales to relate to people, 'I was a dancing girl for Van der Graaf Generator' might be quite hard to beat. Already a prolific songwriter – if one still very much honing his craft – Hammill had first met Judge Smith when the latter chanced upon him playing guitar and singing one of his compositions. Asked by the impressed Smith how many he had written, his answer was apparently 'about 75'. Not bad for someone just turning 19 years old, all in all. The band name, incidentally, came from a list drawn up by the science-influenced Smith, although the reason for the correct spelling of the Van de Graaff generator machine itself being changed for the band name is unclear. Still, we can be grateful that other names on the list were decided against, as the mooted Zeiss Manifold and the Shrieking Plasma might have been a little dramatic for some tastes.

VdGG played several times for the Student Union around that time, with the shows generally being somewhat anarchic, featuring such delights as Judge Smith playing a typewriter as percussion, setting fire to his drumsticks and chasing people away from the stage dressed as a werewolf complete with dripping blood capsules. It got them noticed, at any rate. The biggest gig they played at the time was when they got to support Jimi Hendrix at the Student Union, but it was to be another show which was the biggest influence on the development of the band; that being when they witnessed The Crazy World of Arthur Brown, in November 1967.

Arthur Brown was already notorious for singing his hit 'Fire' with his head ablaze, wearing a 'helmet' which looked disturbingly like an upside-down sink colander. For this particular show, he also turned up with a broken leg. This would not be unheard of in itself, but the explanation he gave to the *Manchester Independent* newspaper certainly was. According to Arthur, he sustained this injury when, while standing on the edge of a cliff, a seagull landed on his head. This made him overbalance and plummet down to the rocks below, only for certain death to be averted when the Devil, in the form of a conveniently passing shark, recognised him as one of his sons and saved his life. Sadly, in actual fact, he had fallen out of a van. Whatever the circumstances surrounding his condition, the show made a huge impression on the watching Smith and Hammill – in particular, organist Vincent Crane, who would later go on to form Atomic Rooster. Normally the Crazy World had a guitarist, but on this occasion consisted just of organ and drums, but so distinctive was the sound produced by Crane that both Smith and Hammill vowed that whatever happened to the VdGG line-up in the future, it would always include an organist.

After a series of shows featuring a sometimes fluid line-up revolving around the trio of Hammill, Smith and Pearne, along with Wilkinson, the core threesome split from the others and kept the name – with the blessing of Wilkinson, who had initially brought the band together but bore no objection or ill will towards them. Hammill, meanwhile, continued churning out songs, sometimes co-writing with Smith, and several would go on to be used on future recordings. Around this time they acquired their first manager, of sorts – an eccentric electronics wizard named Caleb Bradley, who would fashion amplifiers for the band's equipment by recycling old TVs for the purpose – in a highly dangerous fashion as these makeshift amps would be wired up directly to the mains. Miraculously, no one was electrocuted and, in his most meaningful contribution to the band's story, Bradley arranged for them to record a couple of tracks in a studio. The word 'studio' is a little loose in this context as it consisted of the front room and conservatory of his parent's house near Brighton. Nevertheless, he kitted it out with all of the required gear, although it must be said that, even for the time, one microphone shared between Hammill and Smith, incorrectly wired co-axial cable and a single reel-to-reel tape recorder did not constitute Abbey Road. Still, with Hammill armed with a new Hagstrom ED46 guitar which he had bought (with Caleb Bradley's money) for the occasion, the band went on to commit versions of the songs 'Firebrand' and 'Sunshine' to tape. Even at this point, VdGG were proving anything but the norm, with Pearne deciding to adorn 'Sunshine' with an introductory passage taken directly from Widor's *Organ Symphony No 5* played on harmonium. He later admitted that he had no idea why he had chosen to do this. Bradley sent copies of the demo tape out to several record companies and radio DJs and waited.

During this waiting period, a few things started to happen. The three-piece VdGG played their first gig at the university, headlining what was billed as a 'happening' (as things were back then). Hundreds of people turned up, but the gig was apparently a complete disaster. Keren and Maggie, the 'hippy dancers' took part as well, but nothing could save the evening. At around the same time, Caleb Bradley and Judge Smith both joined the local branch of Scientology and Hammill and Smith played a show as a duo supporting Tyrannosaurus Rex at another Manchester venue. Eventually, one of the fish bit at the demo tape, with Lou Reizner, then head of A&R at Mercury Records, inviting the band down to London to meet up, where they stayed for a week or so hanging with the 'in crowd' as it were, at some of the trendy venues of the time. At the end of that week, they headed down to Littlehampton for a photo session on the beach, arranged by the *Manchester Independent* newspaper, who were taking an interest in the band by this time. The resulting photos are odd, to say the least, Pearne posing with a huge, snake-like, 18th-century wind instrument called a Serpent, Smith with a strange instrument called a Phonofiddle, and Hammill with – for no discernible reason – a Vox guitar covered in rabbit fur and a bust of Wagner.

Caleb Bradley took his leave from the band's employment around this time – after successfully reclaiming the Hagstrom guitar – and went back to his university studies. The band, meanwhile, spent a short time being 'mentored', after a fashion, by Graham Bond, the deeply strange musician from The Graham Bond Organisation who cultivated a heroic alcohol and hard drug habit, became utterly obsessed with the 'White Magick' side of the occult, and finally threw himself in front of a Tube train in 1974. Unless, as some believe, it was murder and he was pushed. He was in a strange phase of his never-exactly-normal life at this point in 1968, but he gave the young VdGG a lot of his time and advice. It was seemingly too much for Nick Pearne, however, who left the band in May 1968, preferring to 'stick to being an amateur', and went back to his studies full-time. The pair were now actively seeking a replacement keyboard player, and this arrived as a result of a talk with a friend of theirs who had been in the band's circle for some time, Alastair Banton. He recommended his brother Hugh, and with the band having a contract with Mercury, he took little persuading to sign up. The rest, as they say, is history.

****

Hugh Banton was born in April 1949 in Yeovil, Somerset, taking piano lessons from the age of seven, before the family moved north to Edinburgh in 1961. Hugh ended up attending a public school in Yorkshire called Silcoates, where he took to a rather grand Walker pipe organ in the school chapel with great enthusiasm. In his latter days there, he took up the position of 'school organist', playing for all the chapel services, and studying the instrument with a teacher, Percy Saunders, who was also the organist at Wakefield Cathedral.

On leaving the school in 1966, he went to work for the BBC for a while, while switching his musical allegiance to becoming a Hendrix-influenced guitarist. In fact, in a similar way to Hammill and Smith, it was seeing Vincent Crane play in early 1968 which set him on the road to being a rock organist. He actually became friends with Crane later, as his wife Sue and Crane's wife-to-be Jeannie had known each other since before meeting Hugh and Vincent. Hugh and Sue were guests at Vincent and Jeannie's wedding in 1977, and in fact, took the wedding photographs. An undeniably brilliant musician, Vincent Crane suffered for years with bipolar disorder, and tragically took his own life in 1989, at the age of 45.

Banton was already developing a keen interest in modifying his own instruments, and it became a regular sight in his flat to see an organ stripped down and in the process of being rebuilt in *Frankenstein* fashion. When he first joined the band, he borrowed Judge Smith's Farfisa Compact Duo organ and set about cannibalising it to install rotating speakers in the manner of the famous Leslie system, and hooking it up to a distortion box and another amplifier. Judge never did get the instrument back!

Another bizarre photo session was arranged by Mercury, again down on the south coast, this time with Banton dressed, oddly, as Beethoven, while Smith modelled an authentic-looking Dracula cape in dramatic fashion. This was only marking time, however, and it was clear that they had to find new management and also expand the line-up. Banton, as the newcomer, was dispatched to drum up management interest and new musicians, armed with another demo tape recorded just before his arrival by Smith and Hammill. Touting around a recording you didn't even play on must have been somewhat dispiriting, but nevertheless, tout it he did. The first thing he did was to head to the offices of the counter-culture magazine *it* (International Times) to see about placing an ad for musicians wanted. He met the advertising manager and, while placing the advertisement, also obtained a list of useful phone numbers. He called all of the numbers but got nowhere except for Tony Stratton-Smith, with whom he secured an appointment. 'Strat', as he was always known, liked the tape and agreed to take them on. He would soon, of course, start up his own record label, Charisma, and was also managing The Nice, featuring Keith Emerson, at this time.

In the meantime the ad for musicians ran in *it*, though it was entirely useless. Intended to be for a drummer and guitarist, it actually read 'need organist, bass and guitarist' which, since Banton was himself the new organist and also had designs on playing bass himself using organ pedals, he had, in effect, advertised for his own job. The band also elected not to use a guitarist at all, which makes the whole thing completely redundant and a heroic failure. In fact, their first new recruit came from Stratton-Smith – and it was indeed a bass player.

Strat had gone into band management in the mid-1960s, having earlier been a sports journalist, and one of the bands he represented were a Liverpool group called The Koobas, who spent around six years appealing to almost nobody in the UK, despite touring the country with The Beatles and The Moody Blues in 1965. Their bass player, however, caught the eye of Strat, who recommended him to his new VdGG charges after The Koobas split up in 1968. His name was Keith Ellis. As a side note to this, the first band Ellis joined after leaving school was another Liverpool group called Vince Earl and The Talismen. While they never even released a record, interestingly, bandleader Vince Earl went on to be an actor, most famously playing the character Ron Dixon in the soap opera *Brookside* for a couple of decades – thus providing an unexpected 'what's the connection between...' quiz question!

So they were four, but a drummer was still urgently required, and this duly arrived, for all future incarnations of the band, in the shape of Birmingham-born Guy Evans. Born Guy Randolph Evans in June 1947, he took up a course in Economics and Sociology at Warwick University in 1965 – the first year it opened. A drummer with a keen interest in jazz as well as blues and popular music, he joined his first band during his second university year. Now, just in case you happen to think Van der Graaf Generator is something of an unwieldy name, spare a thought for Guy's band, who went under the snappy banner of The Fixed Price Keynesian Economic Model. Indeed. They did later shorten the name to The New Economic Model, which was marginally better, but would have still been likely to see them having their lunch money stolen by tougher bands. There were also seven of them, which, ironically, was not at all economical. They only lasted two years. Guy then joined a 'psychedelic power trio' called The Green Marble Mind, who bizarrely played at Germaine Greer's wedding party but appear to have done little else. To put this into context, Greer was a lecturer at Warwick University at the time. The psychedelic distractions of The Green Marble Mind do not appear to have done much for the happy couple, as the marriage lasted all of three weeks.

At this point, having completed his degree and done time keeping the wolf from the door driving a lorry and laying kerbstones, Guy was introduced to VdGG by a contact at *it* who remembered them looking for a drummer. He travelled to London and auditioned at Hugh's flat above an ice cream parlour. The audition was not exactly a wild success, with the band not thinking Guy was as good as he thought he was, and Guy not thinking the band were as good as they thought they were. In the exhaustive biography *Van der Graaf Generator: The Book*, Guy memorably described his first impressions thus:

> My hopes that I might hook up with some kind of credible jazz/blues powerhouse were confounded by the spectacle of a falsetto choirboy with an endless supply of material veering between mutant pop and weird shit about the supernatural, a very odd second singer who constantly switched between vocals, ocarina, slide saxophone and stuff in a bag, a church organist playing a Farfisa Compact Duo and a bass player who looked like he'd stumbled in by mistake from the Star Club. I liked them enormously but didn't hold out much hope of persuading them to play some proper music.

Despite these musical reservations, the fact that Guy and the band got along so well straight away overrode any doubts and he took the position. Now they were five, but before too long, they would be four again.

Strat had arranged for the band to record a single at Marquee Studios by this time (October 1968), consisting of the songs 'People You Were Going To' and 'Firebrand', to be released on Tetragrammaton Records. The

15

recording was quite successful, with Banton unusually playing guitar on 'Firebrand' (a Fender Mustang), but Judge Smith was starting to realise he was becoming a little surplus to requirements. The band's sound had now become significantly heavier and more professional, and his – as he put it – 'hippy nose flutes and typewriters' were no longer required. He also had ceased playing the drums, and so began to see his role as little more than a backing singer. Admirably, he stepped aside from the group he had been instrumental in founding, and left with his pride intact and no ill feeling. Occasionally, he will reappear in this story. But now, once again, they were four.

****

The new band's first gig ended up in farcical disaster, in an event which surely must have given them all manner of gloomy portents for the future. Securing a booking back in Manchester, they set off from London in a transit van, only for them to suffer a puncture on the M1 and have to be rescued, as they had no spare. During the long wait for assistance, Hugh Banton needed to relieve himself, stepped over a wall for privacy and promptly fell down a sheer drop onto a railway line. Amazingly he escaped serious injury other than to his pride, and a chastened band all trooped in to Strat's haunt at the La Chasse club to explain that they had spent about seven hours on the M1 and missed the gig.

Things soon picked up after this inauspicious beginning, however, with gigs starting to be played in notable venues such as a show supporting Yes at the Marquee (even if they were amusingly billed on this occasion as 'Van de Graff Generation'), while on 18 November they were invited to the BBC (Banton's old employers) to record a radio session for *Top Gear*. It was aired on the 29th by John Peel, who by now was becoming enamoured of the group, and comprised the tracks 'People You Were Going To', 'Afterwards', 'Necromancer' and 'Octopus' in their first recorded incarnations.

With the Tetragrammaton single finally being released on 17 January 1969, the band made another vital contact when they met up with influential venue MC and DJ John Anthony at a show at the Speakeasy in Central London. Things seemed to be going from strength to strength, but once again, things conspired against them when, following positive reviews for the new single, it emerged that Hammill and Smith were still under their old contract with Mercury Records. They promptly threatened legal action and the single was withdrawn. Undeterred, the band went back into Marquee Studios to record another two songs in the hope of a single release; versions of 'Afterwards' and 'Necromancer'. The producer was John Anthony – beginning his association with the band in that role.

The band were certainly pressing on with their plans and not looking back following the burying of the Tetragrammaton single, so one might hope that at this point in the story fortune might smile on the beleaguered group. Unfortunately, at the end of January, their van containing a whole pile of their gear was stolen. It is believed to have been taken while parked outside a hotel in Paddington, though this is not conclusive but what is beyond doubt is that neither the van nor its contents were ever seen again, despite a reward of £100 for information leading to its return being offered via an announcement in *Melody Maker*. One casualty of the theft was Judge Smith's Farfisa organ which Hugh Banton still had officially on loan, and another was Banton's Fender Mustang guitar. Guy Evans was badly hit as two drum kits were in the van. This led to the cash-strapped band having to play gigs on borrowed equipment as best they could – a situation not relished by any of them but especially not by the 'mad professor' Banton with his home-modified equipment. He remembers playing a couple of gigs with borrowed keyboards (a Vox Continental for one show and a Hammond A100 organ for another), and playing different instruments for each show was clearly an entirely untenable long-term option. Guy Evans had managed to borrow a drum kit belonging to Bob Henrit – later to find success with Argent – so he was marginally better off. Banton, at the end of his tether with the situation, managed to wheedle money out of Strat for a new Farfisa Professional organ, bought just ahead of a show at the Speakeasy.

If all this sounds as if life in VdGG at this point was perpetually glum, this wasn't always the case, as Guy Evans has told of a show at University College in Central London, where they all travelled separately and met up at the venue. Keith Ellis, who was there first, led them up to the dressing room, which was on the fourth floor. On entering the room, Ellis suddenly announced in dramatic fashion that he could go on no longer and immediately jumped out of the window. Clearly, this alarmed the others, until it was discovered that Ellis – an inveterate practical joker – had already realised that there was a ledge just below the window!

Things looked up for real soon after this, when – in an echo of that early Jimi Hendrix show at Manchester University – they had been given the chance to open for Hendrix again, only this time at the far more prestigious surroundings of the Albert Hall. The only drawback was that the gig was such short notice that they found out on the same day, and had to travel there immediately. Less time for stage fright to develop, at least, one would imagine. Also on the bill, in between VdGG and Hendrix, were Fat Mattress, featuring Hendrix's old Experience bassist Noel Redding, and by all accounts, VdGG – in stage clothes hastily bought that afternoon in Kensington Market – went down pretty well. They didn't get the chance to meet the headliners, which is a shame as the show turned out to be Hendrix's last UK show before his Isle of Wight Festival appearance the following year, shortly before his untimely death in September 1970.

The band continued playing shows up and down the country, but the problems with the still largely unreplaced gear continued. Added to this were increasingly sour relations with Mercury Records, who were at odds with Stratton-Smith, to say the least. He felt that the deal signed with them by the Hammill/Smith/Pearne line-up was a very poor one, and as a matter of principle he refused to let Banton, Evans or Ellis sign with them. Mercury for their part believed that they should have the whole of the band by default by virtue of the earlier contract, but Strat would have none of this. There was therefore a situation whereby only one of them was signed to Mercury, but they could not sign with anyone else as a band because of this. Thus the 'Afterwards' / 'Necromancer' would-be single had not been released and, worse still, Mercury banned the group from making any more recordings until the matter was resolved, which frankly didn't look likely without the imminent involvement of a UN peacekeeping force.

With this impasse added to the continuing strain of using borrowed equipment (with the exception of Banton's organ), the band decided – for the first time but certainly not the last – to split up following one last show. Peter Hammill remembered this in the later CD compilation release *The Box*:

So not only could we not record, but we had no equipment to play. Strat was in the States with The Nice and the Bonzos [Bonzo Dog Doo-Dah Band], so we were completely kippered. But we did do one final show using borrowed gear at Notts County Football Ground.

That show in Nottingham was in fact, a festival which took place on 10 May 1969, compered by John Peel and Ed Stewart. As well as VdGG, there was a tremendous line-up of acts, including Pink Floyd, Fleetwood Mac,

Love Sculpture, Status Quo, Georgie Fame, The Keef Hartley Band and, somewhat incongruously, the Tremeloes. Most of the VdGG equipment was borrowed for the performance from The Keef Hartley Band, but despite this – or perhaps even born out of the frustration – the band reportedly played a very intense and dramatic set, and received calls for an encore from an impressed crowd, as opposed to their merciless heckling of the hapless Tremeloes earlier in the day. Still, there was no going back for now, and John Peel reluctantly informed the crowd that they had just witnessed the final VdGG show. Or so everyone thought...

****

Having thus gone, for the moment at least, their separate ways, the Van der Graaf men busied themselves to greater or lesser degrees with other work. Peter Hammill began doing a regular half-hour slot at a weekly Friday Night 'midnight until dawn' show at the Lyceum in London; known as 'The Midnight Court', it often featured other up-and-coming or established names such as Yes, The Nice, The Bonzo Dog Doo-Dah Band and Renaissance, with several of these regular bands having connections to the ubiquitous Tony Stratton-Smith, who seemed to have his fingers in more pies than there were pies at the time; and with things such as Charisma Records, began inventing his own pies! Hugh Banton, meanwhile, was less busy, having had auditions for a few bands, without any of them leading to anything concrete. These included Wishbone Ash as it happens – a band who famously pioneered the twin-guitar sound with no keyboards, so it's interesting to speculate how things might have been different had that union come about! Guy Evans, meanwhile, got involved with a band called The Misunderstood – a link which would directly impact the future of VdGG soon afterwards.

The Misunderstood were a psychedelic band originally from California in 1966, who had gone through line-up changes, a split and a reformation, with various members being respectively drafted into the US military or deported back to America from the UK. By March 1969, the two men who by now constituted what remained of the band, singer Steve Hoard and guitarist Glenn Campbell (no, not that one), were in London again. After a short-lived line-up including ex-Nice guitarist David O'List on bass collapsed after releasing a hopelessly titled single 'You're Tuff Enough', Guy Evans ended up joining, along with a 16-year-old bassist called Nic Potter, who would soon enter the VdGG story himself. The Misunderstood seemed to be on a trajectory, making that of VdGG seem almost mundane, playing gigs at venues as absurdly different to one another as the Royal Albert Hall and the teen fashion department in Harrods in the same month. That Albert Hall appearance was notable as it was as part of an event called 'The Pop Proms', at which they appeared amid a near-riot. They were opening for Chuck Berry, who was headlining that day (and, as Guy confirms, also for The Who the following day), and wild scenes between Mods and Rockers broke out – although one would have thought such rivalry was defunct by 1969. Not so in this case, as the appearance of Berry attracted a large number of hardcore old biker/rockers and The Misunderstood played their set accompanied by sharpened coins, cans and even bicycle chains raining down on them. By all accounts, they went down well, so we can only imagine the scenes had they not done so …

By this time, Keith Ellis had got together with Suzie O'List, David's sister, and they were living in Islington. Knowing The Misunderstood guys, he took a trip over to Germany with them as they were to make a TV appearance over there, an event which redefines the phrase 'stranger than fiction'. Hoard and Campbell, the cornerstones of the band, had both been refused entry to Germany for the recording, leaving the band as just new recruits Potter and Evans. The band's manager, Nigel Thomas, wasn't going to let a small thing like having no band stop him, however. They would be miming, so he devised a cunning plan to use Keith Ellis as a stand-in for Campbell and future Juicy Lucy singer Ray Owen as Hoard. They may have been miming, but there still appeared to be notable holes in this plan, not least that Ray Owen was black and Steve Hoard was white. The appearance was performing the 'You're Tuff Enough' single, and so the spectacle was of these four people miming to a song that none of them had appeared on. They got away with it, unbelievably, but the triumph didn't last long, as Nigel Thomas took them out to a pricey restaurant in a limousine, explaining over dinner that he had incurred huge debts while over there and they should immediately run for the airport! He sent them off in separate cabs, saying he would meet them there, and after waiting with some concern for quite a while, Thomas rushed in, explaining that he was in a little trouble and they should head for the plane straight away. They did so, only to be confronted by a group of German policemen as they tried to board, pointing machine guns at them and shouting, 'Halt!' They halted. Having been taken to a room containing not only the police but also all of the people Thomas owed money to, somehow he got away with paying them off, using all the money they had earned from the TV appearance. As soon as they got back to London, Thomas announced that there was no need to worry, as he had another plan, which was to attempt to sell the story to the *Daily Mirror*. He did try this. They didn't get rich from the proceeds, and The Misunderstood ceased to be after a final show on 3 August. As Guy remembers the incident now:

> The thing with Nigel Thomas was that he was a sort of old-school 'public school' rogue, and he used to take delight in being outrageous and exploiting situations to the hilt. He could be very charming with people, and as soon as we got there he fixed up these chauffeur-driven Mercedes cars for us and all that, somehow persuading people that they would be paid for. When we were heading out onto the tarmac at the airport, as you used to do, this great convoy of police and restaurant owners and all of that arrived. When they brought all of the creditors into the room to face up against him, it was incredible!

In the meantime, other things were afoot in Van der Graaf land, as Peter Hammill was planning to record a solo album at Trident Studios in July, and he invited Banton, Evans and Ellis to come along and record it with him.

Despite the previous ill feeling between the band (and particularly Strat) and the label, the album was set to be released on Mercury. When the band split up, Peter Hammill found himself in a simpler position, as the only one still signed to Mercury, and things seemed to be on a much more even keel for a while. With the exception of 'Afterwards' and 'Necromancer', which had already been recorded for the would-be single, the rest of the album was completed in two days, over 31 July and 1 August 1969 (technically recorded in two months, but actually 12 hours plus mixing!), and was produced and engineered by John Anthony and Robin Cable – the first album assignment for both of these soon-to-be significant talents. The album title was to be *The Aerosol Grey Machine* (as also was the short but rather funny title track), which is a nod back to Judge Smith's time with the band. The story is that when drinks were quite often spiked with LSD by nefarious university characters, Smith was rather concerned about it as he had what was reportedly a very low tolerance to any hallucinatory drug such as acid. Hammill jokingly suggested that Smith might need an 'aerosol grey machine' which could counter the effects of such consciousness-altering drugs by making everything artificially grey.

The resulting album, when released in September, emerged as the debut release from Van der Graaf Generator rather than the intended Hammill solo recording because it became clear to the musicians when recording it that to all intents and purposes, this was the band, and they simply coalesced together once again. However, it wasn't quite as simple as that – is anything ever simple in the VdGG universe? – and by the time they convened for rehearsals as a reconstituted band again, they were a five-piece with just three men from the album remaining.

When The Misunderstood split after their final gig on 3 August, Guy Evans jumped at the chance to return officially to the Van der Graaf fold, but Keith Ellis had other ideas, instead throwing his hand in with three of The Misunderstood members to form another band, Juicy Lucy, who had some moderate success. Things didn't go well for Keith, however, as in time, he was dismissed from Juicy Lucy and split from Suzie O'List, before bouncing from musical job to job. He met and married a girl named Deborah in 1973, but after a spell in the band Boxer, he sadly died from an overdose in his hotel room following a show with a re-formed Iron Butterfly in December 1978 at the age of 32.

Back in 1969, his departure from Van der Graaf led to a need for a replacement, and that man was Nic Potter, Guy's old bandmate from, once again, The Misunderstood. Already familiar to the band, one jam session and he was in. The other new position was less straightforward, though in the context of the band, far more significant. Jeff Peach had played flute on the track 'Running Back' on the album, and the band liked the idea of the extra lead instrument. Peach was offered the permanent job, but backed out of it at the 11th hour before his first rehearsal, so other avenues had to be pursued.

Meanwhile, *The Aerosol Grey Machine* came out on Mercury in September, but only in the USA at that time. Mercury were scaling down their UK and European activities, and it never did get on their release schedule, while predictably in America where they had zero profile, it sold a negligible amount. All in all, it is an interesting album, but was already out of date and unrepresentative of the band even by the time it came out. Highlights include the beautiful ballad 'Afterwards' and the lengthy pair of 'Aquarius' and 'Octopus' (the latter being perhaps the closest precursor to the darker sound the band would begin to cultivate from then on). One song, 'Orthentian Street', was split into two parts, but rather than for any musical significance this was merely because money and time to mix it all together ran out! The odd song title, incidentally, comes from a roadie's mispronunciation of the name Athenaeum Street in Sunderland while asking directions to the venue for that night's gig. Another odd fact on the first pressing of the album was that the track 'Necromancer' was replaced by 'Giant Squid', which was mentioned on the sleeve but was not in the tracklisting. This error was corrected on the next pressing by reinstating 'Necromancer', but rather than just adding it, it replaced 'Giant Squid', which then simply dropped off the album completely. The squid would remain in the picture, however, being played regularly on stage along with 'Octopus' in a medley for some time. They really should have called it the 'Seafood Medley', in retrospect...

Back to the search for a new instrumentalist for the line-up, and it was time for Judge Smith to enter proceedings once again. Since leaving the VdGG orbit, he had been playing with a band called Heebalob and, when he played some demo tracks for Peter Hammill, the latter was impressed by the band's saxophonist (who also played the flute), David Jackson. When Hammill played on the same bill with Heebalob at the Plumpton Jazz Festival on 9 August, he was even more taken with Jackson's playing and, when Heebalob soon called it a day, their loss was Van der Graaf's gain when Jackson (born in 1947 in Stamford, Lincolnshire) was offered the job as member number five. The line-up was now complete, and the new band began rehearsing in September at the exotically named Workers' Co-operative Society Rooms in Notting Hill Gate. The record label worries were also removed when Stratton-Smith set up the Charisma label, with the aim to reach what he called in *Voxpop* 'the student market, all the drop-outs, the fringe people... not a *Top of the Pops* audience'. Which just about summed up VdGG, who, along with The Nice and Rare Bird, constituted the initial Charisma signings. Soon after, they would be joined by another disparate bunch with Lindisfarne, Monty Python, Audience and the fledgling Genesis coming on board. The stage was set for the entry into the 1970s of both band and label and, right at the beginning of that decade, what was considered the first 'proper' Van der Graaf Generator album.

1970 – Not Drowning, But Waving

The Least We Can Do Is Wave To Each Other

Personnel:

Peter Hammill: lead vocals and acoustic guitar (piano on 'Refugees')

David Jackson: saxophone, flute and backing vocals

Hugh Banton: organ, piano and backing vocals

Nic Potter: bass guitar, electric guitar

Guy Evans: drums and percussion

Additional personnel:

Mike Hurwitz: cello on 'Refugees'

Gerry Salisbury: cornet on 'White Hammer'

Recorded at Trident Studios, London, December 1969

Produced by John Anthony

Released: February 1970 (UK: Charisma, US: Probe)

Highest chart places: UK 47

Running time: 43:50

Tracklisting:

1. 'Darkness (11/11)' (Hammill) 7.28, 2. 'Refugees' (Hammill) 6.23, 3. 'White Hammer' (Hammill) 8.15, 4. 'Whatever Would Robert Have Said' (Hammill) 6.07, 5. 'Out Of My Book' (Hammill, Jackson) 4.08, 6. 'After The Flood' (Hammill) 11.27

H To He, Who Am The Only One

Personnel:

Peter Hammill: lead vocals and acoustic guitar (piano on 'House With No Door')

David Jackson: saxophone, flute and backing vocals

Hugh Banton: organ, piano, oscillator and backing vocals (bass guitar on 'House With No Door' and 'Pioneers Over c')

Nic Potter: bass guitar

Guy Evans: drums and percussion

Additional personnel:

Robert Fripp: guitar on 'The Emperor In His War Room'

Recorded at Trident Studios, London, June–November 1970

Produced by John Anthony

Released: December 1970 (UK: Charisma, US: Dunhill)

Highest chart places: Did not chart

Running time: 47:15

Tracklisting:

1. 'Killer' (Hammill, Smith, Banton) 8.24, 2. 'House With No Door' (Hammill) 6.37,

3. 'The Emperor In His War Room' (Hammill) 8.15, 4. 'Lost' (Hammill) 11.17, 5. 'Pioneers Over c' (Hammill, Jackson) 12.42

In the latter part of 1969, the newly re-formed five-piece VdGG did play a few live shows –including their debut, where they appeared with Heebalob on their own final show, in the somewhat unlikely location of Clapham Transport Museum (which has almost certainly never been lauded as 'the rock and roll capital of the world'), but the majority of their time was spent preparing and rehearsing new material for the next album. While they would play some of the *Aerosol Grey Machine* songs live, clearly, there needed to be something more representative of the new instrumental line-up, both for live performance and on record. The album, which would be titled *The Least We Can Do Is Wave To Each Other*, was recorded over a period of four days in December – twice the length of its predecessor, but still hardly Pink Floyd with *Wish You Were Here*!

This time, fortunately, the label was Charisma and consequently, the album was released in the UK. In fact, it came out in February, with the US release on Probe Records being a little later on a date unspecified. It came housed in an eye-catching gatefold sleeve – if somewhat DIY in appearance to be honest – featuring the ball of a Van de Graaff generator machine itself (in a somewhat literal way), emerging out of the sea with lightning crackling from the top of it and the faces of the band in a tiny window in the ball itself. Following the lightning to the back shows the band themselves adrift on a raft, sitting around a candle for no obvious reason. The inner gatefold has head shots of the members next to photos of each of them as children, along with the candle again, with what may be a 'Frankenstein' face mask together with some marbles at the foot of it. Amusingly, the obvious budget nature of the cover photo session is revealed by the fact that in the photos on the inner spread, they are all wearing exactly the same clothes as they are on the raft – so we can at least assume that they returned safely from their watery excursion! The sleeve notes include the dedication: 'To L & M, without whom everyone would have been so much happier', which rather pointedly refers to Lou Reizner and Mercury, making its point in a rather obliquely satisfying way. The title (as well as the cover concept) comes from the quote 'We're all awash in a sea of blood, and the least we can do is wave to each other', sometimes incorrectly ascribed to John Milton but is in actual fact courtesy of the artist John Minton – a bohemian figure in post-war London art circles who passed away in 1957 at the age of 39.

The album itself, consisting of only six tracks, is a massive leap forward from the previous album, both lyrically and, especially, musically. It opens with 'Darkness (11/11)', which is as powerful a statement of intent as one could imagine, showing the music immediately taking the very darkest of turns in line with the song title. Dealing with Hammill's ruminations on fate and the seemingly hopeless nature of it all, it opens with howling wind (sourced from a BBC Sound Effects record), before the band gradually come in, leading to Hammill's vocal, pushed over into the left channel. The music and the vocal both rise and fall in terrifyingly intense synchronicity, with the stereo panning of the voice and instruments particularly effective. This is especially true when listened to on headphones, which brings into uneasy prominence moments such as the line 'Bless the baby, born today', which is answered quietly in the right channel by the grim caveat 'Wicked little Scorpio, doomed to die a thousand times before he lives'. The song ends in dramatic chaos as the pleading line 'Don't blame me, please, for the fate that falls' gives way to anguished repetitions of 'I did not choose it', with the final coda showing for the first time just how important Guy Evans' inspirational drumming could be, as he performs rolls and fills which lift things to another level. This is the first appearance of the 'real' Van der Graaf Generator, black in heart and red in tooth and claw, and it is stunning even today. The 11/11 subtitle stems from Hammill's keen interest at the time in the study of Numerology, as he later wrote in *Killers, Angels, Refugees*: 'It was composed on the night of 11 November 1968, Remembrance Day, by chance… November is, of course, the month of Scorpio, under which sign I was born, and my life number is 11. It was, I suppose, inevitable that a song about fate should be wrought amid these conjunctions. To this day, I do not know how Hereward the Wake came to be involved' (this last comment in reference to 'Boats burn the bridge in the fens' in particular, which alludes to the siege of Ely, and Hereward's actions).

Following that is, as on both sides of the record, a gentler song sandwiched between two slices of intensity, in this case, the classic 'Refugees'. Sung in unusually sweet tones by Hammill, who somehow manages to sound naïve, world-weary and inspiring all at the same time, it deals with the aching regret caused by leaving familiar friends and surroundings for pastures new, along with also the hope engendered by that same move and the possibilities it contains. The characters 'Mike and Susie' refer to Hammill's old flatmates in London, Mike being Mike McLean and Susie being the actress Susan Penhaligon, who will both turn up again in another song later in the decade. The track features David Jackson's flute, and also a cello part written by Hugh Banton, which is played by guest musician Mike Hurwitz, both of which are perfectly judged. Still one of the band's most celebrated songs, there can be few examples of a piece of music which manages to express nostalgic longing and brave hope for the future simultaneously and in quite such an inspiring way.

For the climax to the side, however, we return immediately to the dark side for 'White Hammer', referring to the *Malleus Maleficarum*, the infamous 15th-century treatise on witchcraft and its persecution, written by the terrifyingly demented clergyman Heinrich Kramer, and essentially the 15th-century version of 'The Spanish Inquisition For Dummies'. The song draws from this tome's ghastly recommendations of various forms of murder and torture to weave a picture of the 'White Hammer' of the title bringing doom to both the 'black' and 'white', or 'evil' and 'good', forms of magick, should such a thing exist – and also the inferred damnation of those who would wield this power. And you thought 'I Don't Like Mondays' was a rather harrowing true story! Following the declamation of this grim history lesson, the music fades out before returning in utter howling chaos to bring the side to a conclusion. But never fear, there's still a second side to go at yet ...

The second half of the album opens with 'Whatever Would Robert Have Said', in which the 'Robert' of the title tips its hat to Robert Van de Graaff himself, though that doesn't tap into the lyrical content all that much, which deals with contradictions in nature and the human condition, full of cheery lines such as 'I am the hate you still deny, though the blood is on your hands'. Even Peter Hammill has commented that the relevance of Robert to the lyric now escapes him. Quite a complex song in structure, despite its relatively short duration, it also features Nic Potter on electric lead guitar in a remarkably effective way since he couldn't actually play the instrument! Or at least, he didn't know he could as he had never tried before. An electric guitar was found in the studio and, being encouraged to try it, he simply played it with his fingers in exactly the way he played the bass, and somehow conjured up very effective lead lines, which add a lot to the song. Not for the first time, Van der Graaf Generator demonstrated that they were resolutely not like other bands.

The gentle meat in the gloomy sandwich this time is 'Out Of My Book', written by Hammill with David Jackson, and the only piece not solely written by Hammill. It is as close as the band ever got to a straightforward love song, its very pretty instrumentation dealing with the effect of the passage of time and the ageing process on a romantic couple. As Peter Hammill later wrote, somewhat obliquely:

> This song makes reference to an unfortunate school experience, the allocation at the start of term of a maths textbook in which the answers to exercises are absent. Although working from an answer to a question is a dishonest way of approaching a scientific, as an emotional, problem it is disturbing to know that there is no 'escape clause', and that the only way one can arrive at an answer is by logic. In such an illogical emotional area as the context of this song, the disturbance itself can seem greater than the disturbing factor, the question.

Which may or may not clarify things.

It's a very nice song indeed, and a welcome respite, but I think by this time, everybody is ready for a ghastly 11-minute depiction of an earth destroyed by an apocalyptic flood caused – rather prophetically – by climate change, and dooming us all to oblivion at the hands of our own arrogance. No? Ah well, you're going to get it anyway, as it's time for the album's closing *pièce de résistance*, 'After The Flood'. The tale related in this monstrously dramatic and magnificently overwrought tale refers to a great flood caused by the polar ice caps melting, which engulfs the earth. When the waters eventually recede, no life is left. Five decades later, this has attained a startling relevance which goes beyond mere curiosity and practically into the realms of prophecy, since to most people in 1970, the concept of 'global warming' would have probably meant little more than a spell of nice weather making for a pleasant day on the beach. Having essentially brought the matter of climate change almost single-handedly into the world of popular media, Hammill, and indeed the whole band, give it a treatment which pulls no possible punches in terms of its terrifying threat. Albert Einstein is quoted towards the end of the song, in a spoken word section which reads 'Every step appears to be the unavoidable consequence of the preceding one, and in the end there beckons more and more clearly, total annihilation', with that final word stretched out in an agonised cry with a robotic 'Dalek' treatment which could inspire nightmares if listened to in the dark. This is followed by the closing section, in which the intensity builds with repetitions of 'And when the water falls again, all is dead and nobody lives' (if one wanted to be pedantic, it could be pointed out that if all are dead, then it would naturally follow that nobody lives, but that would be rather churlish). This was dark, dark stuff indeed, and of course, there would be no respite if the listener wished to start the album again, as then 'Darkness' would enter the picture again. Van der Graaf material would over time, become grimmer still, but this was certainly some start.

There was also a single version of 'Refugees' which, rather than being a simple edit of the album track, is actually given a new orchestral arrangement by Hugh Banton, with some of the vocals also mixed higher. It didn't help it make the charts, of course, but it's a nice alternative version. The B-side to the single was 'The Boat Of Millions Of Years', a song drawn from Hammill's fascination with Egyptian mythology. In fact, on the single, it is incorrectly titled 'The Boat Of A Million Years', which is out by, well, millions of years. It was given its correct title when it appeared on the compilation album *68–71*.

After the final mix of the album was completed, Strat decided, for whatever reason, that he didn't think it was as good as it could be, so he went ahead and made the unilateral decision to bring in producer Shel Talmy (a friend of his) to remix it. Now, Talmy was undeniably one of the most respected record producers around, having made quite a name for himself with The Who and The Kinks. However, with the work he was known for, he was also very much more of a specialist in 'mono' production, and there is a great deal of difference between a mono Who single and the sort of stereo madness swirling around tracks such as 'Darkness'. As a result, his apparently 'sounding great in mono' mix was loathed by the band, who objected in the strongest possible terms. The situation was muddied by the fact that an oblivious John Anthony, aware that the original master disc, done at HMV in Oxford Street, was plagued by some sibilance issues – which is that 'hissing' sound which can be so grating when present on pronunciation of the letter S – had himself personally supervised a new remastering job at Trident's brand new mastering facility. In the end, this new version was used to the ultimate satisfaction of all parties, but the Talmy mix was actually in the shops for a very short time before being hastily withdrawn.

On its release, the album exceeded everyone's expectations by actually making it into the UK album charts. Okay, it was only number 47, which didn't exactly make it *Dark Side Of The Moon*, but for a relatively new and very uncompromising band such as VdGG, it was a tremendous achievement. The reviews were overwhelmingly positive, and the band's stock found itself rising considerably, giving Charisma, on the whole, a leg up in terms of visibility as a consequence. All of this led to the next development in the 'stranger than fiction' Van der Graaf story: an offer to do a film soundtrack...

****

The film in question was a British thriller called *Eyewitness*, starring Mark Lester, Susan George and Lionel Jeffries. Lester played a boy who witnesses a murder while on holiday, is subsequently targeted by the killers but is met with disbelief and cynicism by the authorities owing to his habit of inventing his own fantasy worlds – essentially, it's *The Boy Who Cried Wolf* with a false nose and glasses. In America, for no discernible reason, it was released under the wildly irrelevant title of *Sudden Terror*, but it made little difference as the film's box office performance in both markets made lead balloons seem positively wind-borne by comparison, despite the strong cast.

Interestingly, the Van der Graaf involvement came about courtesy of no less a cinematic luminary than Jonathan Demme, later director of *Silence of the Lambs,* among many other impressive successes. At the time, just a young music journalist, he was asked to help source likely bands for the soundtrack, and as it happened, he was a huge VdGG fan, having written about the band in glowing terms in a magazine called *Fusion*. Taking the assignment seriously, he looked at the film's requirements and decided to recruit two bands to provide very different kinds of soundtrack content – VdGG were, unsurprisingly, given the task of producing the more sinister and terrifying music for the violent and shocking scenes, while the jollier, more upbeat and frothy moments would be accompanied by music from British psych-pop band Kaleidoscope – not to be confused with the far superior US band of the same name. The UK Kaleidoscope rebranded themselves around this time as Fairfield Parlour, under which name they were credited in the film.

The Van der Graaf contributions were certainly startling and arresting – indeed, perhaps too much so, as the makers of the film were apparently alarmed at the terrifying nature of some of the sounds delivered to them. The syrupy and safe composer David Whitaker was brought in to submit some bits of music to be substituted for moments when the VdGG cacophony became too much for those with a delicate disposition. This ended up as 'most of it', sadly. Whitaker, incidentally, was later responsible for the ghastly assault on Buddy Holly's

'Heartbeat', sung by actor Nick Berry, which infested the higher regions of the UK singles chart in the 1980s after featuring as the theme music to the family-friendly TV show of the same name. It can be said with some confidence that he represented about as much of a polar opposite to the VdGG outpourings as it would be possible to get. A very small amount of Van der Graaf music survived to the final cut of the film, generally to accompany moments during which a horrible murder is being perpetrated, which seems about right. It makes an interesting watch now for fans, but since it is rarely screened these days, it should not be regarded as remotely essential viewing. Even at the time, ironically, the film had very few 'Eyewitnesses' itself!

This new filmic career having turned out to be a heroic failure, the band went back to their stronger suit and began playing a string of live shows from April onwards, both in the UK and, increasingly, in mainland Europe as well. Before this activity, however, they had travelled to Germany for a TV appearance on the well-respected (if hopelessly named) programme *Beat Club*. With Jethro Tull in the studio at the same time, in Bremen, Van der Graaf treated viewers to scorching renditions of 'Whatever Would Robert Have Said?' and 'Darkness' – which would, in all fairness, be among the last things you would expect to hear in an actual 'beat club'! The live shows were becoming utterly uncompromising by this time, and Hammill said later, in an interview with *National Rockstar*, that large swathes of the audience would walk out of every gig they played. 'People who come and see us now know what to expect. But for the first few years, whenever we played a place for the first time, you could guarantee that 30 per cent of the audience would walk out.' These disgusted or shocked patrons contrasted sharply with the other end of the spectrum, as Hammill remembered when speaking to *Mojo* that 'there would be people in the front rows who were just kind of transfixed and bug-eyed'. Which is a polarising effect which sums up the spirit of Van der Graaf Generator, and indeed Peter Hammill himself, better than I ever could. One particular show at the Festival Hall in London, organised as a Charisma showcase by Strat (with Audience in support), saw the band refuse to bend to the sensibilities of any important music business types present, and perversely yet unsurprisingly triggered a mass walkout by droves of audience members with an utterly uncompromising set. One contemporary review by Chris Welch described the performance by including the phrase 'appalling saxophone and "dustbins-of-my-mind" type lyrics', which is harsh yet amusing.

To be fair to some of those encountering the band on all cylinders and unprepared for the attack on their senses, Jackson's saxophone must have been hard to come to terms with, as he had by now begun playing the instrument in a totally electric manner – that is to say, wired up rather than simply pointed at a microphone which would be the normal way. He would regularly play two saxophones at once in a specially constructed harness, putting them through an effects board more at home with an electric guitarist, including wah-wah, echo, distortion, phasing and even an octave divider. This was something which was as far from the traditional 'horn section' as brass instrumentation could possibly get, and effortlessly gave the band the new element to their sound that they had been craving.

The band were by now able to get bigger and better gig bookings, including two festivals in Germany during July, at Aachen and Munich. Several of the bands travelled over together on the same flight, and what they found greeting them at the airport was somewhat bizarre, to say the least. Senta Berger was an Austrian-German actress who was a huge star in Germany at the time, and something of a national sex symbol – and for no reason which is immediately apparent, she was there on the runway to greet the musicians, accompanied by a brass band.

One would doubt whether Ms Berger would have had much in the way of appreciation for the work of Van der Graaf Generator, but then again, who can tell, as the band seem to have been the toast of the future Hollywood directorial scene. Following their soundtrack recommendation by Jonathan Demme, they attracted another movie-bound uber-fan in the shape of Anthony Minghella, who would later go on to direct *The English Patient*, for which he won Academy Awards for Best Director and Best Picture. In 1970, as a teenager, he was obsessed with the band, following them around from gig to gig and later admitting that he would eulogise about them to anyone who would listen at the time. Once again, this can be seen to sum up the VdGG career in a nutshell – attracting famous and influential admirers a mere 30 years too early...

The band did receive an invitation to record a session for the BBC, which was done in front of a live studio audience and broadcast on 2 August. The band performed three tracks: 'Whatever Would Robert Have Said?', the 'Seafood Medley' of 'Squid 1 / Squid 2 / Octopus' and a track from their upcoming album, 'Killer'. All three were barnstorming renditions, and again did their growing reputation no harm at all.

In between live duties, the band had begun work on the next studio album, road-testing some of the new material in live shows as it was written. This time around, rather than recording everything in a frantic burst of activity over a few days, they were taking their time, going into Trident Studios every now and then to get something new down on tape. By August, three tracks were already done, and everything was looking very good indeed. Then came yet another bombshell as Nic Potter announced, right in the middle of recording the album, that he was leaving the band. All those involved stress to this day that there was no animosity, and most of the cause for the decision was simply that Potter was more of a straight rocker at heart, and did not entirely connect with the complex and unconventional material that VdGG were producing. However, he also said later that his being the youngest member and feeling the need to settle down with a new girlfriend were also secondary contributors. The reasons may well have been understandable and fully accepted, but the timing was most certainly far from ideal. It would appear that he must have given some notice before up and leaving, as the gap between his last show with the band (8 August at the Plumpton Jazz Festival) and the next scheduled gig was only a week, and realistic logic would dictate that contingency plans must have been in place, but reports (and memories) of the time are sketchy and contradictory at best.

Whatever the timeline, the band clearly had to get a replacement in with some haste. This presented itself in the shape of a ready-made candidate who was regularly playing football with the band. They used to play five-a-side quite often against a team from the band Brinsley Schwarz, featuring a young (and still hirsute) Nick Lowe. One of their roadies at the time, who regularly played for the Brinsleys' team, was also a bass player on the lookout for a band. His name was Dave Anderson, a veteran of two albums with the German band Amon Düül II, and he was duly invited to an audition. Not expecting to be successful owing to the significant number of other hopefuls with as much or more experience, nevertheless he was offered the position. Delighted by this, he went to a rehearsal session with the band, which turned into something of a disaster when their tea was spiked with acid and things became strange and – reportedly – not exactly pleasant, or indeed conducive to practical work. Nevertheless, all seemed fine until the band had something of a change of heart and instead offered the job to another candidate. Namely, Hugh Banton's feet.

Hugh had, of course, contemplated handling the bass parts on pedals before, and this time the plan came to fruition. Part of the thinking in arriving at the decision was not only that he could do it – being an experienced church organist, playing with foot pedals was second nature to him – but more the fact that he felt that he had more control over that element of the sound if he handled it himself. In having a separate bass guitarist, it was another variable with which both he and Guy Evans had to work, as a sort of 'middle man', but with him supplying the bass parts – albeit in a somewhat simpler form than the lines which a bass guitarist could play – it was one less variable in the already fearsomely complex house of musical cards which was Van der Graaf Generator on stage. Still, one can only imagine that it must have been disappointing for Dave Anderson to learn that he had narrowly lost the audition to someone's feet.

Once again, there was no rancour in the situation. Personality-wise, all of the band agreed that Dave fitted in well with them as a 'family' and, indeed, after losing out on the position, he actually asked whether he could stay on as roadie while he found something else, which he duly did. When he did leave, it was to take up another position on the very periphery of the mainstream, as he joined Hawkwind, replacing Thomas Crimble, who had come in following their debut album but did not last. Anderson played on the following album *In Search Of Space*, before being replaced by Lemmy later the same year. He would go on to play with a number of Hawkwind spin-off projects over the years, as well as The Groundhogs.

The first order of business for the now four-piece VdGG was to obtain a new instrument for Hugh Banton, and Strat was persuaded to open the Charisma purse strings for a new Hammond E112 organ, complete with a full set of bass pedals. Hugh would still play the Farfisa organ for certain parts, but the Hammond immediately became his main tool of choice, naturally. Equally predictably, he set to modifying it and attaching fuzz boxes and all manner of additions and tweaks in his own uniquely 'Frankenstein' way. Alongside the entirely electric saxophone arena that David Jackson was now inhabiting, the Van der Graaf sound was becoming unlike anything else being attempted within the progressive rock field at the time. Not only did they have keyboards and brass instruments which now sounded at times as if they had marched out of the gates of Hell and taken their place among the living, but apart from the occasional bits of acoustic guitar which Hammill would play from time to time, they were now an entirely stringless band. There were other bands who operated without a guitarist, but doing without a bassist either was pretty much-uncharted territory. However, uncharted territory was where Van der Graaf lived, so all of this was grist to their musical mill.

Hugh Banton says now of the E112, in a fascinating explanation of his various instrumental configurations:

First gig with organ pedals was on 15 August 1970 in Folkestone. This probably remains the most revolutionary VdGG organ: my main object was to be able to get independent effects on each keyboard, so that I could play the distorted solos – which litter our early work – on one keyboard, but accompany them with regular clean organ chords on the other keyboard and on the pedals. Or alternatively, to play two separate fuzz lines at the same time. Not normally possible on a Hammond!

I retained the Farfisa organ alongside as a third and very non-Hammond organ manual, mainly for the ethereal effects on numbers such as 'White Hammer', 'Lemmings' etc., but also using it as yet another distorted solo sound source when required. I also rewired the Hammond motor switch so that I could run the organ's generators down while keeping all the internal valve circuits live: cutting the motor in and out with distortion and echo devices in circuit leads to delightful sonic chaos!

The amplification also became complex: I generated a stereo 'Leslie' effect through the use of two Rotosound boxes with separate amplifiers. The bass pedals had their own amplifier and reflex speaker, built by Nic Potter. I also built a valve-based stereo spring reverberation unit, using Hammond parts, amplified through its own pair of loudspeakers which, wherever possible, were located wide of the stage for 'surround' reverb effect (sadly left behind at a northern gig during 1971 and never seen again). This organ set-up evolved incrementally, hence my well-deserved reputation for 'regularly taking the organ apart'.

During October and November, the band undertook their first major tour of the continent, and also completed the final two songs which were required for the forthcoming album, with Banton actually playing some bass guitar on the recording, though he would have to reproduce everything with his feet in the live arena. By the end of November, it was complete, and in December 1970, the next Van der Graaf album, the confusingly titled *H To He, Who Am The Only One,* was released.

Immediately more accomplished in its cover design than its predecessor, the album featured, for the first but not the last time, artwork by Paul Whitehead (who would also go on to produce the

Nursery Cryme and *Foxtrot* album covers for Charisma labelmates Genesis). The painting adorning the front may need some explanation, appearing as it does at first glance to be some kind of giant pocket watch, set of wheels or disturbingly rendered pair of kidneys, suspended far above the earth along with a peculiarly positioned pair of legs. In fact, the painting – which had already been done as opposed to being a new commission – was entitled *Birthday*, and the wheels/kidneys/halves of a watch actually represented the star sign Libra, or The Balance. This was Whitehead's own star sign, and the beam of light heading down to earth is supposed to be hitting the ground in London and representing his own birth. It isn't his best work, to be fair, but it is certainly eye-catching. The inner gatefold painting, with two hands seemingly about to manipulate a galaxy, is perhaps a better image, and is in fact, entitled *Checkmate*, and in this case, was done especially for the album. Its inspiration was the line 'fingers groping for the galaxies' in the track 'Pioneers Over c'.

The album title might also benefit from some explanation – and in fact, this is itself addressed in rather scholarly fashion on the album's back cover. The H to He referred to is actually a reference to Hydrogen and Helium (and not 'he' as pronounced 'hee'), and the album's note states, 'The fusion of Hydrogen nuclei to form Helium nuclei is the basic exothermic reaction in the sun and stars, and hence is the prime energy source in the universe', accompanied by some fearsome chemical formulae. So, there you are. As for the remainder of the title, 'Who Am The Only One' this is a little more obscure, but in the absence of a definitive consensus on the odd grammatical construction, would appear to be deliberately shifting from third to first-person, indicating that H to He, in a sense, encompasses all of us, and in essence defines our being. Or possibly not. One thing is for sure, it's typically Van der Graaf!

The album opens with 'Killer', a defining statement of intent similar to 'Darkness' on the previous album, but much more dynamic and – for Van der Graaf – direct. Opening with a crunching riff courtesy of Hugh Banton – who would later admit that the inspiration was 'Brontosaurus' by The Move, the lyric tells of a fearsome fish which dwells alone in the dark at the bottom of the sea, killing any other fish which dare to come near it, and consequently doomed to always be alone. This is resolved later into a metaphor for the protagonist's own life, as he himself pushes away and destroys any love or affection shown to him, leaving himself in a destructive vicious circle of loneliness. It's a happy tale. In fact, Hammill had the lyric written a couple of years beforehand, and this does show a little, as lines such as 'you can't have two killers living in the same pad' are rather awkward, not to say dated. Any shortcomings in the lyrical department are outweighed by the musical content, however, which is magnificent. Delivered in an impassioned and tortured way by Hammill, the opening riff section gives way to a 'middle eight' of sorts' which leads on to another riff which is even more propulsive, with a definite swing and swagger to it. It's all very, very intense stuff. The middle section (the 'Death in the sea' vocal part) actually comes from a song Judge Smith used to perform with Heebalob called 'A Cloud As Big As A Man's Hand', and earns him his songwriting credit on the track.

Straight up next comes a complete contrast with 'House With No Door', featuring Hammill on piano and Jackson on flute, which comes closest to the gentle nature of 'Refugees' or 'Out Of My Book' on *The Least We Can Do*, though lyrically it comes from a much darker place. The house with no door is another metaphor for a man withdrawn from the world by his own psychological issues, and illustrates the gradual worsening of his own isolation and dissociation from society. Hammill, by this time, was in very grim territory indeed with his lyrical subjects, and there would be little respite from this approach in the immediate future – to the delight of a huge part of the fan base, who were eating this stuff up joyously.

The final track on the first side of the album is the stark and uncompromising 'The Emperor In His War Room'. Divided into two sections, entitled, rather prosaically, 'The Emperor' and 'The Room', the song tells of a despotic ruler who has sunk into tyranny and cruel depravity after believing his own legend as the 'Saviour of the fallen, protector of the weak'. His descent into corruption is luridly related with such striking lines as 'You crush life in your fist, as your heart is kissed by the lips of death', until finally, his own inner sanctum, his war room itself, is breached by revolutionaries from his oppressed people, with the message to the erstwhile leader being 'Live by sword and you shall die so, all your power shall come to nought / Every life you take is part of your own: death, not power, is what you've bought'. The music here is remarkable in its drama and jagged power, with contrasting serenity here and there to magnify the effect, and Hammill's voice distorted in terrifying fashion at times. Guy Evans admitted later that he did not really care for the piece, as it forced him to inhabit a place in which he was not comfortable remaining for too long: 'Yes, I did feel like that a bit. It was just a little bit too unrelentingly dark, I think.' There is, unusually, lead guitar on the song, contributed by special guest Robert

Fripp, who had loved the previous album and hence agreed to do this session. He reportedly came in, listened through once, and played two takes of a blistering solo (but no more), which were double-tracked to brilliant effect. In *Killers, Angels, Refugees*, Hammill later expressed these reservations about the piece:

> In retrospect, I feel that these lyrics have one particular failing: in my efforts to illuminate the life of the tyrant, horrific images bred and grew out of themselves so that they became self-justifying, rather than explanatory. However, the matter was largely out of my hands, as the elements involved hang on the edge of memory (race or otherwise) and therefore have tendencies to self-direction. I can only hope that the system works in reverse.

He needed to have no such qualms, as the song is possessed of great dramatic import, and the lyrics – while occasionally taken in a very direct manner – detract not one iota from the message or impact of the piece.

The second side contains just two lengthy tracks, the first one being the extraordinary 'Lost' – lyrically at its conceptual level as close to a straight love song as Hammill had written by this time – which nonetheless twists and turns musically from elegiac grandeur to rapid-fire and complex confusion and anguish. An example of prime, 'difficult' VdGG, it is one of the most obvious cases of a track which at first confounds with seemingly jarring and almost dissonant musical sections shoehorned together, until ultimately resolving itself in the listener's consciousness such that those wildly juxtaposed sections could not be imagined in any other way. Even the end of the song does not play out as expected – seeming to finally coalesce into the stately conclusion as an impassioned Hammill finally casts off his self-doubt, pain and unease to triumphantly declare his unequivocal love, before taking one further detour into instrumental chaos which fades away (becoming ultimately literally 'lost'), leaving the inference that all will not end quite so comfortably. Divided once again into two sections ('The Dance In Sand And Sea' and 'The Dance In Frost'), it is one of the most challenging VdGG pieces, at least up to this point, but is endlessly rewarding.

Finally, closing the album is Hammill's grand 'sci-fi' epic 'The Pioneers Over c', which sprawls over around 13 minutes of running time. It is the grim and disquieting tale of the titular pioneers, who are the first men to travel faster than the speed of light (expressed as c, thus the lower-case letter in the song title). This being a hypothetical concept, Hammill envisages a chilling result as the hapless space travellers are lost to time and space as we know it, taking on an existence of their own, beyond our laws of physics, simultaneously doomed to endless death and endless life. Once again, Hammill commented in the *Killers, Angels, Refugees* book:

This is my only attempt at writing a specifically sci-fi song, although the balancing is much more towards fiction than science. Man's first plunge into the unknown territory beyond the speed of light... The Pioneers – the first hypernauts – are, because of theoretical deficiencies, thrown into time-warp or absolute relativity, in which they exist as 'creatures' of limitless imagination but total non-physicality. They are thus potentially ghouls, ghosties, poltergeists and all manner of indefinable Forces: this is one possible explanation, but, truly, in such circumstances, explanations are meaningless, irrelevant and totally speculative. My only regret is that I found it necessary to provide a certain chronological continuity in order to remain, if faintly, within the bounds of comprehension. I don't pretend that there are any answers here, and any questions are entirely subjective.

The chronological continuity he mentions refers to the opening line 'Left the earth in 1983' – dating such a timeless tale somewhat too literally, especially as we are now 40 years on. However, in a song which takes such twists and turns of tense (all past, present and future are now as one to the pioneers) and abstract existence, such small concerns are not significant. In musical terms, the piece is a triumph, unravelling itself gradually and mysteriously over its considerable length, and was very much a product of increased studio technological capability. Trident had by this time gone up to 16-track recording, which gifted far more possibilities in terms of sonic experimentation, and various effects (or 'gimmicks' if you prefer), such as Hugh Banton's oscillator, were used to convey the sense of reality drifting in and out of phase. At one point, a wholly dissonant and unaccompanied saxophone passage drifts along becoming more and more tied up in itself, as it turns into a backwards-recorded sample (illustrating the horrifying shredding of physical and temporal reality). It was rarely played live owing to all of these constraints, and was in its purest form a studio-bound experiment, but it remains a very significant piece. Note that Hugh Banton plays bass guitar on this, one of the two tracks recorded after the departure of Nic Potter (the other being 'House With No Door').

Taken as a whole, the masterful *H To He* makes up one of the most profoundly depressing listening experiences it is possible to imagine. Not in the almost cartoon-like black misery dealt in by the likes of Leonard Cohen or other purveyors of self-absorbed anguish. Rather, it is possessed of a gradual, seeping sense of soul-sucking ennui, coming to a natural conclusion in the tale of the Pioneers, and their eternal, hideously existential 'living death'. I have known times when I have played this album through and, for the rest of the day, found myself possessed of a mild yet undeniable sense of inescapable, nebulous gloom. It is, put simply, a remarkable achievement.

Sadly for the band, the general public did not seem quite as enamoured of the album as they had been with *The Least We Can Do*, and *H To He*, scandalously, failed to chart. As with a number of VdGG recordings, time has been kind to the album, and it is now widely recognised as the triumph which it surely was, with *Q* magazine, three decades after the first release, looking back on the album as consisting of 'portentous, bleak declamations on the human condition', and praising the 'thick, dark layers of organ and saxophone'.

With 1971 just around the corner, it was time to get out on the road and promote the release.

1971 – Lemmings, Angels, Lighthouse Keepers

Fool's Mate (Peter Hammill)

Personnel:

Peter Hammill: vocals, piano, acoustic guitar

David Jackson: saxophone, flute

Hugh Banton: organ, piano

Guy Evans: drums, percussion

Robert Fripp: electric guitar

Martin Pottinger: drums

Nic Potter: bass

Rod Clements: bass, violin

Ray Jackson: harp, mandolin

Recorded at Trident Studios, London, April 1971

Produced by John Anthony

Released: July 1971 (Charisma)

Highest chart places: Did not chart

Running time: 44:28

Tracklisting:

1. 'Imperial Zeppelin' (Hammill, Smith) 3.36, 2. 'Candle' (Hammill) 4.16, 3. 'Happy' (Hammill) 2.36, 4. 'Solitude' (Hammill) 4.56, 5. 'Vision' (Hammill) 3.13, 6. 'Re-Awakening' (Hammill) 4.01, 7. 'Sunshine' (Hammill) 3.56, 8. 'Child' (Hammill) 4.25, 9. 'Summer Song (In The Autumn)' (Hammill) 2.13. 10. 'Viking' (Hammill, Smith) 4.44, 11. 'The Birds' (Hammill) 3.38, 12. 'I Once Wrote Some Poems' (Hammill) 2.56

Pawn Hearts

Personnel:

Peter Hammill: lead and backing vocals, piano, pianet, acoustic and slide guitar

David Jackson: saxophone, flute and backing vocals

Hugh Banton: organ, piano, mellotron, synthesizer, bass guitar and backing vocals

Guy Evans: drums, percussion and piano

Additional personnel:

Robert Fripp: electric guitar

Recorded at Trident Studios, London, July–September 1971

Produced by John Anthony

Released: October 1971 (Charisma)

Highest chart places: Did not chart

Running time: 45:08

Tracklisting:
1. 'Lemmings (including Cog)' (Hammill) 11.35, 2. 'Man-Erg' (Hammill) 10.19, 3. 'A Plague Of Lighthouse Keepers' (Hammill, Banton, Evans, Jackson) 23.04

While the *H To He* album may not have sold enough to trouble the UK charts in any way, it nevertheless did the band's career trajectory no immediate harm, as the reviews were generally enthusiastically favourable, and the hardcore VdGG audience seemed to be expanding. *Sounds* called the record 'a remarkable album', which 'has tremendous drive and energy, and a compelling force behind it which seems to well up from the depths', before noting that the band 'come close to the inventive magnificence of King Crimson'. Al Clark, writing in *Friends* magazine – while making the mistake of calling this the second album by 'the Van der Graaf Generator', concluded his review with: '…play this in the dark with the speakers wide apart and it's devastating. They're the kind of band who might have invented stereo had it not existed already.' *Melody Maker* ran a short feature with Peter Hammill talking about the album, including the rather spurious claim that when he took it to Stratton-Smith's old (and supposedly 'haunted') house, the spirits present refused to allow 'Killer' to be played. Hammill was quoted as claiming: 'The house just wouldn't take 'Killer'. The needle wouldn't stay on the record, and the whole place began to wobble.' Well, they do say that everyone's a critic, but when that gets expanded to include the long-dead, then you know things are getting a bit serious…

There was an early bit of welcome exposure early in 1971 when on 9 January, the band appeared on the BBC2 show *Disco Two*, which would soon evolve into *The Old Grey Whistle Test*. Difficult to find today, it only featured them miming to 'House With No Door', but still, it would have been an invaluable piece of promotion. This, however, was something of a welcome sideshow before the main event got underway, which was the matter of getting on the road again in front of audiences – and, following a few shows in mid-January, this was done in a memorably inspired way owing to an idea by Strat.

Having several bands now signed to Charisma, and liking the idea of showcasing them in a sort of 'package tour' way, he picked out three of the most likely candidates in VdGG, Genesis and Lindisfarne, and put them together on a three-band bill. His brainwave was to price all of the tickets at the low (even for 1971) price of 30p for all three bands – which is six shillings (or 'six bob') in the pre-decimalisation 'old money'.

The tour was then christened 'The Six Bob Tour', and has retained that affectionate title ever since. It was a risky strategy, as a low price like that would have seen the tour lose money if attendances had not been extremely healthy, but the strength of the idea was proven when sell-out crowds were attracted at most of the nine UK theatre venues visited. It may seem hard to believe today, given the way the respective bands' careers panned out, but Genesis were bottom of the bill, opening every show, with Lindisfarne in the middle and VdGG, the headliners. There was one exception to this, in Lindisfarne's home city of Newcastle, when VdGG ceded the headline spot to them so that they could go on last as the 'conquering heroes' on their home turf.

All three of the bands involved have spoken of the camaraderie and friendships which developed between the musicians on the tour, which used a single large tour bus to transport all three bands around. Rod Clements from Lindisfarne remembers that they boarded the bus and, finding Genesis at the front of the bus and VdGG encamped at the back, they did the obvious and went in the middle – but he has said that these demarcation lines were soon broken down as the band members intermingled. Guy Evans and Phil Collins spent quite a bit of time together, sometimes sitting at the back of the bus with their drumsticks, playing together on whatever was available ('Phil had much better technique than me, but I learned a lot,' Guy now says, in rather modest fashion). Peter Gabriel, meanwhile, spoke of getting on very well with his fellow singer and lyricist Peter Hammill, saying that Hammill loved a debate, and had a habit of bringing up controversial topics until the discussion had become satisfyingly heated, which they both relished. There were differences, as Steve Hackett describes Lindisfarne getting deep into a crate of brown ale and wanting a sing-song, while the Genesis contingent would want quiet because they were getting heavily into the *Times* crossword. John Anthony perhaps summed it up best when he said, as quoted in *The Book*, that 'Van der Graaf were in the back rolling joints, Lindisfarne had their crates of Newcastle Brown, and Genesis sat there being uptight!'

The first show of the tour took place at the Lyceum, in London, on 24 January, and right away delivered one of those 'stranger than fiction' occurrences which seem to have been pretty standard fare in the surreality of Van der Graaf World. While the band were setting up for the gig, with Hugh Banton's set of bass pedals ready for one of their biggest outings yet, what should happen? Yes, of course, they fizzled out and refused to work. This being Van der Graaf World, however, it also just happened that none other than Nic Potter was in the audience preparing to watch the show. So, with a bizarre twist on the old 'is there a doctor in the house?' cliché, the situation was effectively 'is there a bass player who was in the band until recently and can play the set from memory in the house?' So, plucked from the audience, Potter ended up playing the show with no notice whatsoever, using Mike Rutherford's bass, which was the only suitable instrument available.

Amazingly, things went roughly according to plan for two whole days after that, before the fates struck again on the way to that evening's show at the Colston Hall, Bristol, and the bus broke down. Stranded on the motorway waiting for assistance to arrive, the bored musicians happened to notice that there was an empty farmer's field right next to the carriageway and – prompted by Phil Collins – proceeded to stage a hastily arranged five-a-side football tournament, which ended up unfinished when the breakdown assistance arrived in time to save the gig but stymie the football!

Against all odds (which I realise seems like a deliberate Phil Collins reference but is honestly not), that evening's show was an exceptionally good one. It has been commented on many times by the band and other witnesses that VdGG shows at the time could be astonishing, but only approximately one in five times. The generally agreed hit rate seems to have been – so 'seat of the pants' were their appearances – that for every five gigs played, two would be okay, two would be disastrous, with one or more of the band having an off night (and/or the gear malfunctioning) and thus affecting the overall improvisational balance, and the remaining one hitting amazing heights as everyone was 100 per cent on their game and bounced off each other brilliantly. That Bristol show was reportedly one of these 'golden gigs', and the band were elated after a performance which had the capacity crowd in raptures. So imagine their surprise when the theatre manager promptly informed them that they were banned from ever appearing at the venue again! The audience, apparently, had 'flouted' the no-standing rule, and this heroically ill-tempered curmudgeon would not have it. In an even greater twist, he actually turned out to be the uncle of Sue Pooley, Strat's secretary and girlfriend of Guy Evans – yet such things clearly cut no ice in his world of 'the people must not leave their seats', and the band were exiled in disgrace from the theatre. Even for Van der Graaf, a catastrophic equipment failure, a farcically coincidental bass player switch, a transport breakdown and impromptu football tournament, and finally a triumphant gig and a ban from a venue, all in the space of the first three days, must have been something of a record.

There were variable reactions to the bands on all of the nine dates of the tour, with Roy Carr reporting on a triumphant VdGG show at Manchester's Free Trade Hall where he described the band as playing 'as if heralding Armageddon' and, even more colourfully, seeming 'to be caught in a self-created astral time-warp' – which I imagine counts as praise. At Newcastle City Hall, there was a near-riot as 500 fans were locked out of the 2,500-capacity venue, and a riot had to be averted. At the Brighton Dome, by contrast, *Sounds* described a show which saw Genesis met with 'audience disinterest', VdGG with 'perplexed torpor' and only Lindisfarne receiving any appeals for an encore whatsoever, with a number of the crowd leaving before the end of the VdGG set. Despite these ups and downs (which were consistent with reports of the range in quality of the shows, in the Van der Graaf case), the tour as a whole was a great success – both for Strat and Charisma, who turned a nice profit, but also for the bands, who all saw their profile substantially increased with the public and in the press. The 'six bob gigs' had proved a 'million dollar scheme', as one might say.

Talking about the tour to Richard Williams in *Melody Maker* at the end of March, Peter Hammill expressed the change which he had personally experienced following the unprecedented ovations they received during the tour:

> I used to feel that I had to go outside myself for an audience, but that's wrong. I thought that I had to make it unreal, in a dramatic sense; now I know that we can make it unreal in a musical sense, taking the people into our little nightmare world. When you've got that kind of motivation, anything can happen.

VdGG went on with some shows of their own as soon as the tour ended, but such had been the demand for, and success of, the 'six-bob' format, a second leg of eight more UK shows was arranged for April. Genesis and Lindisfarne once again made up the bill, but on nights when either were unable to do the show owing to being double-booked, new Charisma signings Bell & Arc stepped in. Bell & Arc were a collaboration between Graham Bell, who had been with Nice drummer Brian Davison's excellent project Every Which Way, and a band called Arc, who had released one album and at one time featured future Yes drummer Alan White in their ranks – but the union lasted for only a single album.

Melody Maker became quite enamoured of VdGG at this time, printing a review of one of the second run of shows by Chris Welch (author of the scathing review from the previous year), who praised the show while using a couple of unintentionally humorous phrases along the way. The audience were described as displaying 'mass enthusiasm' – which sounds like a description of the world's most polite riot – and Hugh Banton was singled out for his impressive use of 'mystery chords', whatever those may be! They also, notably, ran a front-page story on the band (accompanied by a photo of David Jackson), in which the band were described as 'the UK's most fashionable group', which is very hard to credit, even in 1971!

A break from the fairly frantic VdGG activity came in April when Peter Hammill recorded his first solo album, *Fool's Mate*. 'A break' largely because, despite all of the VdGG men (including Nic Potter) playing on the album, it was a rather different listening experience. Far from the bombastic and drama-filled array of long epics on the band's releases, *Fool's Mate* by contrast, contained 12 songs, all very much more personal to Hammill, which dated back to his university days. Two of the songs – 'Imperial Zeppelin' and 'Viking' – were particularly noteworthy as they were early collaborations with Judge Smith, who penned the lyrics for both. The tracks are certainly simpler in construction than the VdGG material, but certainly not in emotional force and variation, with many of the songs being extremely sombre and grim, whilst elsewhere there is at least some occasional degree of lighter relief. One of those lighter pieces, 'Sunshine', is a revisiting of the very same song recorded for the band's first demo tape back in 1968 in Caleb Bradley's parents' living room, which underlines one of the elements which make the album a fascinating listen even today – it represents a sort of 'clearing of the attic' for Hammill, who has said that, had he not recorded these songs when he did, they would most likely have been lost to posterity. Two of the tracks, 'Vision' and 'The Birds' have remained regular features of Hammill solo performances to this day, while 'I Once Wrote Some Poems', the powerfully cathartic album closer, would be performed at band shows for a short while.

The album title, *Fool's Mate*, is of course, a chess term for the quickest possible checkmate that can be achieved, and Paul Whitehead's endearingly Python-esque cover painting strongly references this, as the featured chessboard is in fact, set up in a fool's mate position. Hammill was a chess enthusiast, and the games he would go on to play with Hugh Banton on tour would be so intensely competitive that they sometimes had to be discouraged from playing for fear of discord blowing up within the band. Indeed, Banton has said that he would sometimes spend an entire show with his mind partially wrestling with what his next move would be once they resumed the game following the performance – which is about as far as you are likely to get from the Led Zeppelin travelling hedonistic circus, I think it is safe to say!

Elsewhere in the cover painting, which wraps around the gatefold, are a number of random images which Whitehead has confirmed were, in many cases, long-forgotten in-jokes arising from the studio time which Hammill himself requested to go in there. There are obvious references, such as the Viking ship and the Zeppelin, but elsewhere there are such oddities as a teddy bear, a surfer emerging from the chessboard, a woman shopping and a man with only his bowler hat visible. The section on the back cover has the bizarre image of Peter Hammill's head emerging from a plughole (plug included), while next to that is an assembly line of garden gnomes, a pyramid and a large sign reading 'Keep Left'.

Classic cover that it is, the painting was almost claimed by a freak accident, as Whitehead explained in a 1997 interview with Jim Christopulos and published in the VdGG fan magazine *Pilgrims*:

It was incredibly complicated because each one of those little chess pieces had to be masked and sprayed, so it took me ten days to do that and then do the collage. And I took it to show Peter at the studio and the other guys were there. It was, like, ten at night, we went until two in the morning, got a little high. And I said, 'Great, so I'll get this to the printers…' and off I went. I walked out into the street and at that time, I was driving a little Mini Minor. I put the art work on the roof of the car and off I went! And I'd driven the car about a mile or so and suddenly I had this horrendous realisation: 'Oh shit, I left the artwork on the roof.' I stopped and got out and of course, it wasn't there, right? So I traced back the route that I'd come and I went up the street where Trident Studios was… and the street sweeper was coming the opposite direction with the water going and the brushes and I felt sick… I got almost parallel with the studio and there's the artwork lying face down in the street with mud and tyre marks and scuffs all across the back of it… I picked it up, and what had happened is that the street sweeper made almost like a vacuum. It had pushed the art down into the street and the water had sealed it. So I opened it up, and there wasn't a mark on it… So I stood there and I had this devilish idea. I went to the studio looking down and depressed and miserable and said, 'You won't believe what happened, guys'… And I showed them the back of it, right? Then I whipped up the cover and went, 'But the artwork's okay!!!' We even considered for a while to put the back of the artwork (with the scuffs, mud etc.) on the cover somewhere.

Recorded in eight days at Trident in April 1971, the *Fool's Mate* album was released in the UK in July. Obviously, it did not trouble the charts. It retains a unique fascination, however, standing apart from the rest of Hammill's 1970s solo output in its scope and approach.

In the meantime, as VdGG continued gigging the length and breadth of the country, both on their own and with the 'six bob' brigade, a piece which was to become forever linked to them – for better or worse – was about to enter the picture. Around this time, the band had taken to doing some rather left-field instrumental encores, partly as a way of defusing the heavy angst and tension built up by their regular set. Remembering these encore selections, Hugh Banton says:

'The Dam Busters March' featured fairly regularly. I know the *Star Trek* theme was on the list, but we possibly never perfected it. 'Je t'aime'. 'Carmen'. It was pretty mad – there was also 'Nellie the Elephant', 'Popcorn' and more than one national anthem!

While driving back through the night on one of their lengthy motorway trips (to save on hotel accommodation was an important consideration, even if it meant driving all night), they used to put the radio on to hear Radio 1 when it began broadcasting for the day at 5am. The introductory theme music was an orchestral piece written by George Martin for the purpose, and named – somewhat unimaginatively – 'Theme One'. Liking the piece a lot, they sort of learned it by 'osmosis' from these dawn listenings, and pretty soon, the piece entered the set as a regular encore for a while. The whole encore sequence would begin with Hammill, alone, performing 'I Once Wrote Some Poems' on acoustic guitar and vocal only. When he finished the song, he would exit the stage as the rest of the band entered, and they would launch into a rousing rendition of 'Theme One'. They recorded their version, and George Martin himself voiced his approval – and in fact, in time, it replaced the original as the Radio 1 closing theme at the end of the John Peel show at midnight. It would re-enter the picture in another way shortly.

With the two legs of the 'six bob tour' concluded, Stratton-Smith and Charisma – encouraged by the success of the format – arranged for a tour of Germany to follow the same model. The tickets would be reasonably priced, and VdGG, as headliners, would be accompanied by two of the label's other bands on a communal travel bus (it starts to sound more and more like the plot for a Cliff Richard film by now, one has to say). This time, the accompanying bands would be Audience and Jackson Heights – the latter formed by ex-Nice bassist/vocalist Lee Jackson, and named rather cleverly after an area in Queens, New York. While on paper, it would appear to have been a safe bet for more on-the-road laughs and communal jollity, the reality, this time out would be very different. The tour was arranged by Strat, though he was almost entirely absent from it himself, and as a result, business affairs would start to go wrong. The bands found themselves either not getting paid, or else getting paid in dollars, which they would be unable to spend. They were getting hungry, with little or no money in their pockets, and travelling around on what must have been one of the slowest tour buses ever commissioned, as it struggled to do more than 30 mph, and trips were long and tense. David Jackson found the bus atmosphere so toxic – by contrast to the UK equivalents – that he would regularly travel in the van with the roadies and the gear. Lee Jackson reportedly went one step further, and actually had his car sent over so that he could travel himself. Even the roadies on this trip were not what you would expect – reportedly, there were three of them, two of whom only had one lung, while the dual-lunged third man only had one eye! The shows themselves, meanwhile, were uneven affairs, with the Van der Graaf performances continuing to follow the '1-2-2' ratio of great to average to terrible, though on this occasion, sound issues would often cause the latter, with some shows torpedoed by howling feedback. Hugh also remembers that the Hammond organ was a notorious recipe for disaster when taken on the road, especially in Europe: 'One of the problems was that it depended very much on a stable mains supply, which you didn't get on the Continent.' Germany was a popular territory for the band, who had, of course, appeared on German TV, but while they had a good solid fan base, there were many others at the shows who were unprepared for their sonic assault, especially after being serenaded by the much more approachable sound of the two support bands.

While the tour was a pressure-cooker atmosphere which became highly stressful and unpleasant much of the time, there is a general feeling expressed by the VdGG men that in some ways, it strengthened them as a unit. There was certainly a good amount of 'gallows humour' to leaven the poverty and hunger. Hugh Banton, speaking in *The Book*, tells of one incident which they found hilarious when, at a quiet point in proceedings, a lone voice could be heard shouting – in a very heavy German accent – 'Fukk off vith yor muzik!' He tells how they adopted it as a catchphrase for some time, shouting to each other at random moments: 'Jackson! Fuck off with your music!' – and it is this sort of 'gang mentality' which can easily be imagined to make the foursome even more tightly knit.

Away from the stress and the fatalistic humour, however, Peter Hammill was busily grabbing what solitude he could manage in order to write for the upcoming album. Two pieces, 'Lemmings' and 'Man-Erg' were already complete and being road-tested in the band's set, but what he was frantically scribbling away at was what would become the epic, sprawling 23-minute 'A Plague Of Lighthouse Keepers'. Following the conclusion of the fraught German tour (along with a handful of gigs elsewhere on the continent), the band assembled in Stratton-Smith's old, eerie (and reportedly haunted) Crowborough House to get the material together for the record. This led to a considerable falling-out when Hammill announced the 'Lighthouse Keepers' plan. With two heavy, complex and pretty dark pieces in 'Lemmings' and 'Man-Erg' earmarked for the first side, the other guys (especially Banton) were looking forward to a few short pieces to lighten the mood and ease their creative burden. This idea was quickly killed stone dead in the water by Hammill's announcement that no, he didn't want to do that, because he had put together several disparate parts of a 23-minute monster which would take up the whole of the second side. At this, Banton reportedly threw his metaphorical hands in the air in despair at the plan. Reportedly, Hammill stormed out and went home, only for the rest of the band (who had already agreed to attend a dinner party at his nearby home that evening) to glumly troop over to his house later. In fact, things were smoothed over with the aid of liberal servings of alcohol, and the new 'epic' was embraced by the band. As Guy Evans recalls:

> I don't recall going to dinner at his house, though it is possible, but I certainly do remember him telling us about the piece and thinking, 'Oh no, do we really have to go down this route of making ourselves even more inaccessible to people?' But in actual fact, once we started working on the pieces which made up the 'Lighthouse Keepers' track, I quickly

saw that this was Peter occupying a more abstract place compositionally, and it did in fact, give us more scope to interpret it. So while there was some initial doubt, it changed very quickly.

The album, titled *Pawn Hearts*, was released in the UK in October 1971, enclosed in what was easily the most impressive cover the band had used to date – in fact, many would say the finest artwork they ever had. Once again, a Paul Whitehead painting, the brief he received from Peter Hammill was to illustrate the album title's meaning regarding the fact that whoever we are, and whatever success we achieve, we are all, ultimately, pawns. This was in actual fact, something of a revisionist interpretation, as the story has it that the title originally arose from nothing more meaningful than a David Jackson 'spoonerism' (that is to say, when someone mixes up the beginnings of words when speaking). Jackson had announced one day that he was going to do some 'porn hearts', when he clearly intended to say 'horn parts'. This appealed to the band's sense of humour, and the album title was born. Still, Whitehead could only illustrate what he had been told about, and having listened to 'Lighthouse Keepers' for inspiration, he set about producing the wraparound painting for the gatefold cover. It features an array of people real and fictional, alive and dead, all inside transparent 'pawns', floating above the earth. Behind them, and blocking out the black void of space, is a scrim, or theatre curtain, featuring a cloudy blue sky. Several recognisable characters can be seen inside the pawns: John Lennon, Jesus, Shakespeare, Walter Raleigh, even The Mekon from the *Dan Dare* comic strip. According to Paul Whitehead, Napoleon is on there, but I've never been able to find him. There are a number of characters whose identity may be uncertain, but their roles are clear: there's a cricketer, a few kings, a sailor doing semaphore signalling, a policeman on a bizarre flying ship, an astronaut, a Roman dignitary, an old British soldier in red uniform and a character in a striped shirt who, Whitehouse claims, just represented 'Mr Average'. Some people might be interested to note that, putting the images side by side, in this case, Jesus Christ is definitely bigger than John Lennon, quite literally! There is also a flying saucer and, quite oddly, a flying Jodrell Bank telescope.

If the outer gatefold design is unusual, however, that is small potatoes compared to the truly bizarre photo splashed across the inner gatefold, a weirdly tinted affair which has David Jackson, with an American football under his arm, facing the other three standing on a sloping table, and all four are giving each other Nazi-style raised arm salutes, and wearing black shirts and light-coloured ties. Interviewing Peter Hammill, I asked him to explain this in detail:

Well, the location of that was at a house which Tony Stratton rented in Crowborough, Sussex, which is where we were rehearsing for Pawn Hearts. We had invented a game called Crowborough tennis – one of the facts about Van der Graaf is that we were always inventing strange games, often very physical, if not dangerous! – which involved that table which you see us standing on. The football was bounced off the table in this odd sport which resembled a sort of cross between netball and table tennis. Anyway, the photographer Keith Morris came down to take some pictures of us playing Crowborough tennis, as we were still looking for an inner gatefold spread, and this picture came about at the very end of the session. It actually came from us mimicking a statue which had quite disturbed us when we saw it in Kaiserslautern in Germany, and we took the picture and forgot about it. When the proofs of the photos came through, we just, to a man, said we had to use it, though, of course, there was a degree of how it would be perceived. In the end, we decided that the audience knew us well enough that we didn't embrace any sort of Nazi ethos or anything like that, so we went for it, and that's how that came about!

It is worth noting that, for a Spanish release of the album, the contentious and striking 'Crowborough salute' image was actually used as the front cover image, which really does beg the question as to what they were thinking, as they dismissed the painting which actually related to the title, and instead went straight for the jugular by using a photo which had already courted plenty of controversy just as an inner gatefold spread! Original copies also came with a lyric sheet, and there was a box with credits on the inner gatefold left-hand panel. This came with one entry which would surely have confused most people, with the recording noted as being 'aided and abetted by Nohjndijcrackycracky'. Peter Hammill later noted that this was 'an appalling misprint for Nohjnohjcrackycracky, being a catchphrase for our then roadies, Nohj and Cracky'. So, there we have it.

The album as it was released contained just three tracks – all three of which once again contained some guitar work from Robert Fripp, though not to such obvious or dramatic effect as 'The Emperor In His War Room'. The first side opens with 'Lemmings', a darkly allegorical tale given a level of gravitas when invoking the parallel between human behaviour and the titular cliff-diving creatures. Musically it is by turns imperious and savage, melodious and angular – until it enters the fearsome mid-section entitled 'Cog', which sees the band going just about as far out on the edge of defiant musical abandon and utter refusal to compromise as they had ever done. The opening part of the 'Cog' section, incidentally, comes from taped experiments Hugh Banton had been doing during a visit to his parents' house, recording an electric shaver with all manner of trickery going on. The resulting sounds were dubbed 'the psychedelic razor', and used in the piece as they were. The song proper returns after this chaotic yet oddly thrilling interlude to wrap up the 'story' as it were. 'What choice is there left but to die?' intones Hammill. Quite.

Up next, and occupying the remainder of the side, is the much-vaunted 'Man-Erg', a fan favourite which appears in most VdGG setlists to this day. An examination of the human condition, and the dark and light sides which reside within us all ('killers' and 'angels' respectively), it is a lyrical and musical tour de force. Opening with the quiet rumination of 'The killer lives inside me. I can feel him move...' before the dramatic build into 'but then his eyes will rise and stare through mine, he'll speak my words and slice my mind'. The angels are then referenced with: 'The angels live inside me, I can feel them smile; their presence strokes and soothes the tempest in my mind, and their love can heal the wounds that I have wrought'. This dichotomy can only be contained for so long, however, as the hitherto conventionally melodic and dramatic music is split asunder by a howling sax riff courtesy of Jackson's electrically enhanced maelstrom for the frantic 'Am I Really Me?' section. This gradually resolves back into the opening section of the piece again, as the calm and the chaos battle each other, with the former finally winning out with the affirmation that: 'I'm just a man, and killers, angels, all are these; dictators, saviours, refugees, in war and peace,
as long as Man lives'. It's an extraordinary piece of work, and as close to defining the particular unhinged yet brilliant genius of Van der Graaf as anything can be.

The second side, of course, is given over in its entirety to the aforementioned 'A Plague Of Lighthouse Keepers', which is so far out on the edge as to make the two relatively extreme pieces on the first side sound like a bid for chart success by a glam rock band by comparison. On the face of it, the piece (it cannot by any stretch be merely called a 'song') deals with the lighthouse keeper of the title, haunted by attempts to warn of disaster that he cannot prevent and mixed with the creeping effects of loneliness and solitude to drastically threaten his fragile mental state. 'I prophesy disaster and then I count the cost...', he ruminates, before 'I've been the witness, and the seal of death lingers in the molten wax that is my head'. It only goes downhill from there, as the tale expands to become an examination of the human psyche as a whole, framed by the lone keeper's descent into madness. Over ten sections (all recorded separately before being expertly stitched together by Hugh Banton along with John Anthony), the music veers as sharply and dementedly as the lyrical maelstrom of insanity, lurching from peaceful respite to frenetic chaos and back again, with such bizarre individual subsection titles as 'The Clot Thickens' and '(Custard's) Last Stand'. It all ends with David Jackson's gloriously triumphant music for the closing 'We Go Now', with the lyric finishing on a rather Zen-like and open-ended declamation that 'All things are apart. All things are a part'. So there you have it, pop pickers. Another simple and catchy little number from those Van der Graaf boys...

In actual fact, perfectly constructed as *Pawn Hearts* seems now, it was originally envisioned as a double album. The first disc was to be as the finished album, with the third side being made up of solo tracks, one each from Banton, Jackson and Evans. The fourth side was going to be live recordings, with a version of 'Killer' being mooted. In the end, this plan was dropped and *Pawn Hearts* became the single disc we know today. The unused solo pieces later turned up as CD bonus tracks (or, at least, two of them did), but to be honest, they are inessential. Guy Evans' 'Angle Of Incidents' is an avant-garde experiment, consisting of a host of overdubbed drum parts – many of which were recorded backwards – accompanied by free-form squalling sax. There is also an unexpected interlude consisting of a host of microphones set up to record fluorescent light tubes being thrown down into a stairwell in Trident studio. It can easily be gathered that no tubes survived the experience. There is some nice stereo panning on the drums, but overall, few would want to listen to it more than once. Hugh Banton, unsurprisingly, contributed a collage of organ parts for his piece 'Diminutions'. A rather ambient piece in effect, it does have some nice atmospheric moments, but again is probably one for the curious or the completist. One does get the sense, however, that with work, it could have been developed into something genuinely impressive, and quite possibly rather unsettling, but we will never know. David Jackson's piece 'Agamemnon Agnostic' was never completed, and no recordings remain, which is a shame as it sounds fascinating.

Described by him as an 'anthem in several movements', it was reportedly partly modern classical in tone, and featured lyrics by Peter Hammill, which were in Greek, but it only got as far as a piano skeleton before being abandoned. The aforementioned CD bonus material does contain one solo snippet by him, but it is somewhat less weighty fare, being a sort of jazz pastiche lasting for just under 90 seconds. Nice enough, for sure, but nothing more. There are, needless to say, no Greek lyrics for this one!

The recording of the album (and the planned bonus material) was accompanied by significant amounts of herbal accompaniment, with Hammill, in particular allegedly becoming something of an expert at sticking a host of cigarette papers together to roll vastly constructed joints – conical-shaped creations 'like cone-shaped fireworks' as recalled by Paul Whitehead, while John Anthony tells of 'joints in the shape of a trident – huge architectural things!', which does sound intriguing, to say the least. The band had also taken to doing a little LSD at the time as well, though all concerned claim that the use of acid was an infrequent and well-controlled thing, and there were never any 'bad trips' experienced. It is easy to see how slightly altered states of mind could have fed into the album, however – something only reinforced by Guy Evans' claim that, when he used to pick up Peter Hammill at Victoria Station for recording sessions at the time, the singer had taken to wearing a long rider's coat, like something from an old western film, accompanied by a small white toy policeman's helmet. Things were different in the early 1970s, you see...

There was one more twist in the album's tracklisting, as when it was released in the USA (on Charisma but distributed by Buddah Records), the label had taken it upon themselves to not only add the band's recording of 'Theme One', but also to insert it right in between 'Lemmings' and 'Man-Erg'. The band were naturally unhappy at this decision, especially since the first they heard of it was when the album appeared in the shops. As Peter Hammill put it in an interview with radio station KNAC: '"Lemmings" drifts out and then you get some affirmation after seemingly all hope is gone. If suddenly you've got all hope gone and then there's a jolly tune going in there, and *then* you've got the affirmation, it's rather difficult! So, we aren't always in control...'

While the die-hards were drawn to this dense work like moths to the proverbial flame, critics and the general public were rather more circumspect. When the album appeared in the UK in October, many reviews of the time expressed bafflement about what the band were attempting to achieve, or else simply intimated that they weren't really achieving anything of any note, and sales were disappointing. It is worth noting that time has restored the album to its rightful place as a major work, as it regularly features in retrospective lists of classic albums. The situation wasn't helped by Charisma or, indirectly, Lindisfarne. Charisma were clearly unsure about what to do to market the album, and when Lindisfarne hit paydirt with their hugely successful album *Fog On The Tyne*, they decided to, in fact, avoid the issue by virtually ignoring *Pawn Hearts* promotionally and instead throwing their PR budget in the direction of Newcastle. The Van der Graaf career trajectory graph was by now steadily heading back down towards the X-axis again, though by the band's own admission, almost entirely by their own making as they pursued their own singularly uncompromising muse.

The autumn saw a return in force to the live arena and sustained gigging, but there was to be one more unexpected diversion in December. Recording another John Peel radio session, Van der Graaf Generator did two things that would never have been expected by anyone short of Nostradamus. Firstly, they hooked up with Judge Smith again for the occasion. And secondly, they did it with a comedy Christmas song. This particular five minutes of lunacy, with lyrics and lead vocal from Smith, was entitled 'An Epidemic Of Father Christmases', and it is, literally, about Father Christmas. Opening with a solemn-sounding choral section, the band suddenly enter playing 'Rudolph The Red-Nosed Reindeer', before the song section sees the famously Scrooge-like Smith bellowing out the jolly-sounding chorus of 'Christmas can be terrible, be terrible, be terrible…', as the band plonk away behind him. We then get a bit of Prokofiev's 'Troika', some four years before Greg Lake appropriated it for his own, rather more solemn, Christmas song, before it's a round of 'We wish you a merry Christmas' and close. This curio can be found online for anyone caring to look for it, but be warned, 'great art' it is not!

Thus ended 1971, a year which by any regular band's standards would have been considered a chaotic riot of extreme highs and lows. This being Van der Graaf Generator, however, it was in many ways the calm before the storm which was heading their way in 1972…

1972 – I Prophesy Disaster

Already possessing a fearsome reputation as a 'mad professor' customising his own gear, the end of January 1972 saw Hugh Banton take things to the next level as he spent almost a week in between live shows converting his Hammond organ into something which was to sound utterly unlike any other similar instrument. Following a show in High Wycombe on 22 January, the instrument was delivered to his house by the VdGG roadies, and he had until 27 January (a rehearsal for a show on the 28th) to get it ready. Working through the night on it ('When you go without sleep for two days, you start to hallucinate!', as he remarked in *The Book*) he ended up integrating a whole array of new hardware so that each keyboard and also the pedals were all amplified separately, allowing not only volume levels to be adjusted individually, but also enabling different effects pedals and the like to be applied to each component part of the instrument. By all accounts, the standard of the best VdGG shows was by now becoming even higher, as the equipment began to keep pace with the astonishing invention and innovation of the musicians involved.

In February, 'Theme One' was released as a single, gaining the approval of no less than George Martin himself, who declared himself to be 'bowled over' with the band's version of his piece, describing it as 'a powerful recording that respected the original, but – mixed with their own unique style – created a very contemporary piece indeed. All in all, a great cover version.' On the B-side of the single was a Hammill composition entitled, intriguingly, simply 'w' (in lower case). A short song by VdGG standards, it is musically more intriguing than one might expect from something seemingly relatively minor, and lyrically (containing a reference to a fire at his old school in the line about 'smoke billowing across the lawn'), it ploughs a familiar furrow about the general hopelessness of life and, indeed, death. It is never explained who – or what – 'w' might be, though Hugh Banton offers a suggestion: 'I think it's the idea of a "Double You", hence, "twice as unhappy" etc. But I'm not sure.' Referencing the bagpipe-like sound which opens the song, and as regards 'space beacons' presumably the song's abstract mid-section, Hammill offers the following, somewhat obtuse, comment in the *Killers, Angels, Refugees* book:

'w' is intuitive universal, and it is therefore appropriate that, over the years, it should have been treated with sounds from bagpipes to the bleeping of space beacons. Wave theory is, to me, fascinating but impenetrable, and I now prefer a 'photon' view of life. However, such opinion, when related to such lyrics as 'Darkness', merely proves my own confusion and the potential truth of both.

Which may, or very probably may certainly not, make things clearer. Unless it indicates that 'w' relates to wave theory, which probably doesn't help much in any case...

Also, in February, another significant event happened, which was to shape the destiny of the band for the foreseeable future. With Van der Graaf having achieved some popularity in Italy, a 12-show tour was arranged, their first visit to the country. Following two UK gigs, and a whole day off, they were flying out to Italy, where, in an insane feat of scheduling, they had those 12 shows arranged in a visit lasting eight days. This was achieved by four of the eight venues having them booked to do two shows, one in the evening and another earlier in the day. The tour was all being organised by Italian promoter Maurizio Salvadori, on whom the band would have to rely heavily. A fact which was made more difficult by virtue of him speaking no English and none of the band members speaking Italian. Guy Evans, however, spoke decent French, and as Salvadori also spoke that language, Evans was designated band communicator, in this 'compromise tongue'. That language issue was far from the biggest shock the band would get, however, as from the moment the plane touched down, it became apparent that suddenly, and in a manner more surreal than anything Salvador Dali could have dreamt up in his most fevered imaginings, Van der Graaf Generator were superstars.

It turned out that their popularity had grown into something rather more than they had been aware, with both *Pawn Hearts* and the single 'Theme One' both simultaneously at Number One (with the former reportedly spending four whole months at the top of the album chart). As soon as the band alighted from the plane, they were greeted by scenes which seemed more akin to Beatlemania, with crowds lining the airport and waving flags. David Jackson has said that they were actually looking over their shoulders, thinking that someone else must be behind them! If this was a shock to the system of this cult prog rock band more used to driving faint-hearted people out of their shows, it was nothing compared to the two shows in Milan on 8 February, the first date of the tour, when the crowds of ticketless fans attempting to gain entry required riot police with shields to keep order. The band were bundled in and played the afternoon show to a heroes' reception, but following the performance, they found themselves unable to leave the venue before the evening show, with the hysteria being generated by the hordes wanting to get in for the gig leading to military vehicles joining the riot police and firing smoke bombs and tear gas to disperse the mob! Guy Evans has described it as being 'a full-scale riot', and recalled sitting up on the roof of the theatre watching the madness unfold below. Guy today:

Well, yes, that's right. Though actually, this story has been disputed within the band in more recent times. In fact, Hugh has actually investigated it and come up with the conclusion that there is no way to get onto the roof from within the building! But I certainly have the memory of watching it from up there. I think, looking back, I might have found a way up there with Maurizio and watched it with him, because we had developed quite a friendship at that time.

Armando Gallo, the Italian journalist who penned the Genesis biography *I Know What I Like*, offered his own theory as to how this insane popularity suddenly mushroomed: 'They were very operatic. Their music had dynamics, and everything was rooted in classical music, and the Italians could identify with that. And Van der Graaf had a lot of heart with Peter Hammill. They had these huge crazy numbers, but also things like "Refugees", which was heart-wrenching'. All of which might go some way to explaining why they might find success in the country, but hardly hysteria!

Another factor which put their nerves on a knife edge was the travelling between shows, when they were driven by Maurizio. Anyone who has spent time in Italy will attest to the fact that driving is seemingly often seen as a trial by speed and daring as opposed to a simple mode of transportation, and this was no exception, as Jackson and Evans both recall in *The Book* how Maurizio would gleefully drive at 'terrifying' speed, with his lights flashing and horn blaring to clear the way, while at times steering with his knees as he casually lit a cigarette. It is small wonder that Guy Evans still remembers this with great clarity, as his role as communicator-cum-interpreter meant that he was forced to occupy the front passenger seat at all times: 'Yes, that was a bit hairy! Though I did come to trust him pretty well – perhaps misguidedly! – as he actually was an excellent driver. He had to be to drive as he did and survive, I suppose! He did steer with his knees, there was that – but he did steer very well considering.' Hugh Banton reiterates the driving ability of Maurizio: 'He was actually a very good driver; I think he did rally driving. Things did get a bit crazy at times, but we never hit anything, and at that age, you think you're indestructible! I do have a memory of one bizarre incident when we were on a normal single-carriageway road, and the traffic was backed up nose to tail, and suddenly the whole queue of traffic had the idea to overtake all at the same time. The entire right-hand lane basically moved over in one go to the left, then had to move back again! I've never seen anything like that before or since.' The vehicle in question was an Alfa Romeo Berlinetta, which clearly left an indelible impression on the band's minds, as they released a track some 45 years later reflecting on this madness on their album *Do Not Disturb*. The song title was 'Alfa Berlina'.

Still, one might imagine, at least this automotive terror and the godlike treatment by the populace would have made a change from the more usual Van der Graaf issues of chaotic shows with malfunctioning equipment. One might imagine that, but one would be wrong, as it took only until the second night, in Rome, for Hugh Banton to blow up his organ – or at least for some valves in it to explode during the show. Incidentally, note that the day before, they were playing two shows in Milan. Which means an astonishing 360 miles in the Alfa driven by a knee-steering maniac. No wonder Van der Graaf shows would often be tense affairs. Now, the very next day, there were another two shows in Turin – which, if you know your Italian geography, you will realise is back north towards Milan again, for 430 miles. This means that the band ended up travelling the 90 miles from Milan to Turin, via Rome, for a grand total of almost 800 miles in two days – similar to travelling from a show in Glasgow to one in Edinburgh via Plymouth. Anyhow, having seen parts of his instrument blowing up as he played it, Hugh Banton decided that he would head off with the roadies to find some replacement valves and drive up with them in the band's truck. Having got hold of the required equipment they set off, immediately hit a kerb, and blew two tyres. So, as he remembers it, 'It was, okay, so we've fixed the organ, now we have to fix some tyres.'

Astonishingly, they made it to Turin and the shows went ahead, as did all 12 in this ludicrous eight-day excursion. To make matters worse, the information about the venues they were booked to play at tended to be sketchy at the very best, with roadie Alan 'Granny' Grange recalling that, on arriving in the correct town, their first port of call was to seek out a poster for the show to find out the address of the venue. In fact, he claims that what they sometimes did was to hire a taxi to the venue, and then simply follow it!

Following this breakneck excursion into superstar-land, more gigs around England, as well as in Belgium and France, occupied the band until mid-March, when they played a triumphant sold-out show at the Bataclan venue in Paris (where Supertramp would later record their own live album, itself entitled *Paris*, at the end of the decade). The show was filmed for a French TV show called *Pop 2* (inventiveness was not the stock-in-trade of music show producers at this time, it would seem, with *Disco 2, Pop 2* and *Beat Club* all jockeying for uninspired position – though one does wonder whatever became of *Disco 1* or *Pop 1*). This was naturally a fascinating experience, though not an entirely enjoyable one, however, according to Guy Evans, who remembers huge bulky film cameras (in the days of actual film) being trundled around the stage and thrust into their faces as they played. Compared to the next TV engagement they faced, however, this would be a walk in the proverbial park.

A few days after that Paris show, on 21 March, the band were engaged to play on Belgian TV. The peculiarity about this, according to Evans, was that when doing a music show in Belgium it was generally necessary to film two shows, one for a French-speaking audience and one for a Flemish audience. The French filming was easy, and very much in line with *Top of the Pops,* with the band simply miming to a song whose identity is lost to the ages. It then came time to film the Flemish show, which was entitled *Tienerklanken* – another masterstroke of originality as it translated as 'Teen Sounds'. From that uninspiring title it might be expected that another quick 'mime and you're done' might be anticipated, but far from it. In fact, the producers of the programme, which despite the title seems to have been some kind of serious hippy 'counterculture' presentation, had already arranged to have the band play 'A Plague Of Lighthouse Keepers'. Which they had never played live. The startled band, hearing of this planned performance for the first time, attempted to explain that this would prove almost impossible as not only had the hugely complex 23-minute piece not been played by them for over six months, but they had never played it in more than short chunks at a time when recording it in the studio, and they couldn't actually remember it. This cut no ice, and it was clear that they were going to have to somehow manage this, so they agreed under the condition that they had to take some time to learn it again, and even then, it would have to be filmed in two halves. This was agreed so, after the three-piece went through a performance of 'Theme

One', the band went off for two hours to frantically learn the whole thing again – and have a very cursory rehearsal of it, if any. Amazingly, they managed it, and the performance is as faultless as one could possibly hope for, even if Peter Hammill did have to keep the lyric sheet from the album propped up on his piano in front of him. Surrounded by candles and sparklers in a bizarre setting, the footage is essential viewing as an opportunity to see VdGG at this time up close and personal going as far out on a limb as they could. It may not exactly have been 'Teen Sounds' as one would imagine, but it was a landmark performance.

European performances continued through April and May, with the band touring Holland and Switzerland, including a ludicrous feat of scheduling on 6 May, when they played a show in Bern before a late-night dash saw them drive the 60 miles to Basel for a midnight show there, at a cinema which had gigs on at midnight after films had been shown. Having just played a show and rushed straight from it, they were inclined to change the set rather than simply go through the same one again, but there was no time to plan a different running order. In one of the oddest last-second decisions one could ever wish to see, as they were actually heading on to the stage for the show, Guy Evans suddenly suggested that they play the entire show backwards – and this being Van der Graaf Generator rather than any normal band, everyone immediately agreed. So on a whim, they played the whole show in exact reverse order, opening with the usual encore of 'Theme One' and finishing with the much grimmer dynamics of 'Darkness'. The challenge here, of course, was to make this suddenly reversed pacing work, but by all accounts, it did, though Peter Hammill later described it with some understatement as 'edgy'.

There could be only one thing coming, however, and that was a return to the madness which was the rabid Italian Van der Graaf maniacs, and sure enough, after three more English shows and two in Germany, the band were dispatched there for a second time, from 20 May to 4 June. This two-week tour would once again, almost unfeasibly, comprise 18 shows, as the afternoon/evening double performances returned again on three of the dates. There was one day off on 29 May, as the band took the seven-hour, 450-mile drive from Naples all the way back up to Genoa in the north. This all took place during an oppressive heatwave, with the band members often alighting from the car cramped and exhausted after an all-night drive in the early morning, only to be recognised immediately in the street and surrounded. It was little wonder that tempers were becoming frayed and arguments were beginning to occur.

On one notable occasion, at a show in Viareggio, near Pisa, there was an altercation whereby an audience member grabbed one of David Jackson's saxophones, who promptly hit him on the head with it. After the show, the band had to be bundled into the back of a van and locked in by way of a dressing room, as roadie Alan Grange fended off the milling hordes. The band members (usually Evans and Jackson) were handling their own driving duties this time out, and Evans took the unusual decision to issue a ban on chess playing, as the Hammill-Banton matches had by now started to absorb many of the frustrations prevalent in the pressure-cooker atmosphere, and furious arguments would break out over the slightest contentious move.

By the time this Italian jaunt was over, the band – while having to stop off in Switzerland for a rearranged gig on the way home – were in frazzled disarray. Five more shows followed in June, including another whistle-stop dash over to Paris for a showcase gig with Genesis and Lindisfarne once again, and it is small wonder that Van der Graaf Generator were not in the best of shape. In fact, rumours of a split had begun to be whispered in the music press around this time, though they were refuted. The truth was that they had not decided to split at that time (though Peter Hammill had reportedly flip-flopped on the idea once or twice), but they did have vague discussions about continuing on three fronts simultaneously, with Hammill solo, the band as it was, and also the other three doing things as a trio. It would have panned out a little like Rod Stewart and The Faces, one imagines, but it never came to fruition.

During July, the fractious and road-weary band convened to start rehearsing material for the next album, including the tracks '(In The) Black Room' and 'A Louse Is Not A Home', which would appear on Hammill's next two solo recordings. The work was by all accounts going quite well, with the music being to everyone's taste in terms of its quality and the scope for the band putting their unique stamp on it, but all involved concur that the atmosphere was somewhat less than comfortable. They really needed a break away from each other at this point, but as with so many bands in the hamster wheel of the early 1970s rock world, they weren't about to get it, because the next thing had been lined up for them already, beginning in late July. Yes, another Italian tour, as if the previous two trips into a surrealist's playground hadn't been enough for the beleaguered musicians.

So it was that VdGG left once again for another week in Italy, playing to the adoring hordes, with the seven days from 29 July to 6 August seeing them play an absurd 12 shows. Just to recap, that's 12 shows in a week! They coped manfully enough (Hugh Banton even began playing bass guitar at these shows on a couple of tracks, having purchased a Fender Mustang for the occasion), but the wheels were coming off beneath them, and as soon as they returned to England, the inevitable happened, the rumours were borne out and Van der Graaf Generator disintegrated. The split was officially confirmed internally by letters sent out by Peter Hammill to the other three, but all agree that the band had, to all intents and purposes, ceased to exist in the way it should.

Almost as soon as the announcement of the split became public knowledge, Charisma rush-released a compilation entitled *68–71* – so quickly, in fact, that many who heard it may not have even realised the group had disbanded. With a front cover displaying, rather unimaginatively, the ball of a Van de Graaff generator machine itself, and a rather more interesting back featuring a collage of photos and information as to the tracks and the various incarnations of the band, it was more functional than luxurious in design, but as a sampler, it certainly did its job. The eight tracks were 'Afterwards' and 'Necromancer' from the first album, 'Darkness', 'Whatever Would Robert Have Said' and 'Refugees' from the second, 'Killer' and 'Lost' from the third, and as a bonus for collectors the B-side 'The Boat Of Millions Of Years'. Nothing was included from *Pawn Hearts*, and neither, surprisingly, was 'Theme One' or even perhaps 'w'. The eagle-eyed may note that this means that nothing is included from 1971, and nothing prior to the debut album in 1969, so despite the title, the album is less *68–71* and more accurately *69–70*, though the latter would seem an oddly narrow one for a compilation album title, one imagines.

Another thing which quickly materialised was interest from the Italian market for the non-Hammill trio to record and tour the country. Guy Evans has said he actually got as far as going to Italy to open negotiations about this, with the offer being a contract for an album and tour, but ultimately it failed to materialise. Undoubtedly the three felt that it would be a situation in danger of stepping back into the maelstrom which had just destroyed them, but they also had refused to call themselves Van der Graaf Generator without Peter Hammill in the band, when this was indicated as the preferred choice of the Italian offer.

Hugh Banton quickly got busy recording some instrumental material of his own, some along with Guy Evans – including a piece called 'Brain Seizure' (referring to its baffling time changes), which would

Left: VdGG in 1970, from the same photo session as the US rear cover of *The Least We Can Do*... Clockwise from top: Evans, Potter, Jackson, Hammill, Banton. (*Charisma Press Photo*)

Below: The four-piece, following Nic Potter's departure. (*Charisma Press Photo*)

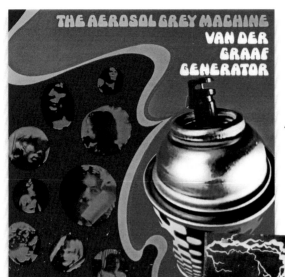

Left: The debut album *The Aerosol Grey Machine,* 1969. (*Mercury*)

Right: *The Least We Can Do Is Wave To Each Other,* 1970. (*Charisma*)

Left: *H To He Who Am The Only One,* 1970. (*Charisma*)

Right: The fascinating gatefold cover to Peter Hammill's solo debut *Fool's Mate*, 1971. (*Charisma*)

Left: *Pawn Hearts* album front cover, 1971. (*Charisma*)

Right: The startling and contentious inner gatefold photo from *Pawn Hearts*, without lettering overlaid.

Left: David Jackson at the Hitfair free festival in Bern, May 1971, when only VdGG played owing to terrible weather. (*Photo – Adrian Haegele*)

Below: David Jackson promo photo. (*Pawn Hearts Society Archive*)

Left: Jaxon on the front page of *Melody Maker*, May 1971 – rubbing shoulders with The Byrds, Rita Coolidge, Laura Nyro, Rod Stewart and Ella Fitzgerald…

Right: VdGG in 1971, near to the Charisma offices in London. (*Charisma Press Photo*)

Above: Onstage at a UK show, date unconfirmed, Spring 1972. (*Photo from the collection of David Jackson*)

Right: Glasgow show on the 1971 'Six Bob Tour'.

John and Tony Smith
in association with
Tony Stratton-Smith
PRESENT

VAN DER GRAAF GENERATOR
Genesis
Graham Bell & Arc
in concert

Greens Playhouse - Glasgow
(RENFIELD ROAD)
FRIDAY 23rd APRIL 1971 at 7.30 p.m.
ALL SEATS 40p ONLY !
Bookable in advance from: Box Office, House of Clydesdale, 160 Sauchiehall St.,
Telephone: 041-332-9572

Printed by Hastings Printing Company, Drury Lane, Hastings, Sussex, Telephone: Hastings 2293/4 & 2450

Top: A wistful – and youthful – looking Peter Hammill, circa 1972. (*Pawn Hearts Society Archive*)

Above: A drawing done by Peter Hammill, which deconstructs how his logo is made up from the letters of his name and the Scorpio sign. (*Pawn Hearts Society Archive*)

Right: Guy Evans at the Hitfair free festival in Bern, May 1971 (*Photo – Adrian Haegele*)

Left: Guy Evans, New Theatre Oxford, November 1976. (*Pawn Hearts Society Archive*)

Right: Guy behind the kit – unknown show. (*Pawn Hearts Society Archive*)

Above: *Chameleon In The Shadow Of The Night* album gatefold cover, 1973. (*Charisma*)

Right: *The Silent Corner And The Empty Stage*, 1974. (*Charisma*)

Left: Guy Evans appearing on an EP with Charlie And The Wide Boys, 1975.

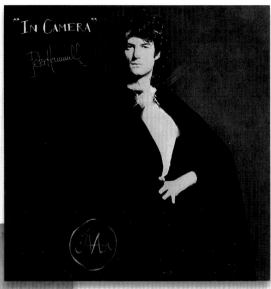

Right: *In Camera,* 1974. (*Charisma*)

Left: *The Long Hello* – the original Italian album cover, 1974.

Right: *The Long Hello* – the rather more minimalist UK cover, 1976.

Above: Receiving a congratulatory cake from the Archduke, Vaduz, Liechtenstein, 1976. (*Pawn Hearts Society Archive*)

Above: Hammill and Jaxon, New Theatre Oxford, November 1976.
(*Pawn Hearts Society Archive*)

(*Courtesy www.vandergraafgenerator.co.uk*)

Right: Hugh Banton, Paris, March 1972.

Left: Hugh Banton with cigarette and shades – 'the undercover man'… (*Pawn Hearts Society Archive*)

Right: Hugh, unusually, on bass guitar – Rheims, 1976. (*Pawn Hearts Society Archive*)

Left: *Nadir's Big Chance*, 1975. (*Charisma*)

Right: *Godbluff*, 1975. (*Charisma*)

Left: *Still Life*, 1976. (*Charisma*)

Right: *World Record*, 1976. (*Charisma*)

Left: *The Quiet Zone / The Pleasure Dome* – 'Quiet Zone side', 1977. (*Charisma*)

Right: *The Quiet Zone / The Pleasure Dome* – 'Pleasure Dome side', 1977. (*Charisma*)

Musik
JOKER MESSE **OFFENBURG**
GELÄNDE

THE SUNRISE FESTIVAL

**WISHBONE STEPHEN
ASH STILLS
BOB MARLEY
& THE WAILERS
THE KINKS WAR
VAN DER GRAAF GENERATOR
MAN**

JUNI '76

Left: Offenburg 'Sunrise Festival' poster, June 1976.

Below: Peter Hammill at an unknown show in 1976. (*Pawn Hearts Society Archive*)

Above: Peter Hammill at the Marquee in 1976. (*Pawn Hearts Society Archive*)

Above: The truncated
Van Der Graaf, five-piece
incarnation L-R: Hammill,
Smith, Dickie, Potter, Evans.
(*Pawn Hearts Society Archive*)

Right: Van Der Graaf gain a
cellist in unlikely circumstances
– Charles Dickie. (*Pawn Hearts
Society Archive*)

Left: Over, 1977. (*Charisma*)

Right: The live *Vital* album, 1978. (*Charisma*)

Left: The bizarrely semi-bearded *PH7*, 1979. (*Charisma*)

emerge somewhat later. He had built a home studio with two two-track tape machines in it by now, so that he could overdub as many times as he wished, by 'bouncing' the tracks from one machine to the other. Interestingly, one thing which Stratton-Smith had suggested to him – which he claimed later to have started but never finished – was the idea of an album based around the theme of Tarot cards. The title of the album was to have been *Voyage Of The Acolyte* – a title (and indeed, theme) which Steve Hackett would later use for his own solo debut, also on Charisma. Hackett's album is so highly regarded even today that one wonders how history might have been different had Hugh completed and released the album. Of course, Steve Hackett's music would still have been recorded, even if the tracks and album might have been differently named, and as the saying has it 'what's in a name' – but even so, it is interesting conjecture. Hugh says about it now: 'Yes, that's quite right, and in a way, I wish I'd completed that. I certainly think I started on it. Strat also offered me a film soundtrack job at the time, and I definitely wish I'd done that one. I'm not sure why I didn't really.' He actually took a full-time job with a PA and equipment hire company called International Entertainment Services at this time, which he enjoyed considerably as it allowed him to continue his technical passion for a living. Sue Pooley was now there (as the boss's secretary, as it happens), so there was a Charisma link, and he knew many of the people he dealt with on a regular basis. With the company developing such things as a quadraphonic PA system for a Yes tour, he would certainly have found the job a home from home of sorts.

Peter Hammill, as one might expect, was very busy at this time, having been considering a split to explore a solo career even before the band imploded. He was living at a descriptively named house called 'Two Green Bushes' in Sussex at the time, with girlfriend Alice and their dog Dylan (who may have been named after Bob, or even the hippy rabbit from *The Magic Roundabout*, who can say), and he was planning to install a home studio in the same way as Banton. He had several ideas on his mind, including recording the songs which had been intended for the next band album along with others he had been intending for himself, but uppermost in his mind was something which would eventually see fruition, but not for a long while. For quite some time, he had been nursing an idea about composing and recording a long-form piece in the manner of an opera, and the catalyst for this came about once again from his old sparring partner Judge Smith. Smith had a long-held idea that Edgar Allan Poe's story *The Fall Of The House Of Usher* would make a perfect musical work, and indeed had started some embryonic work on the words for such a piece while still at school. Hammill was also an admirer of Poe, so he got on board with the idea straight away. Smith managed to unearth his old rudimentary libretto, and it formed a starting point for the pair to begin collaborating on the piece – though it didn't end up as much more than a start, as he later stated that 'maybe one line' of it was eventually used. The work was sporadic, and indeed would continue to be sporadic but never fully abandoned for years to come, until the finished recorded version of *The Fall Of The House Of Usher* finally appeared almost two decades later, in 1991, with all instruments (keyboards, percussion and some guitar) played by Hammill, with a cast of guest vocalists. It is fair to say that it received mixed reviews, with Paul Stump in his somewhat ambitious book *History of Progressive Rock* dismissing it as 'meandering, formless, electronic non-opera at its warbling worst', which probably means he didn't care for it.

The saga of the House was not over, however, with Hammill remixing it, adding more guitar and some violin while removing all the percussion, and releasing a second version eight years later in 1999. It has never been performed live, and after its release, I asked Peter for his thoughts about which he regarded as the 'definitive version':

Hmm – that's a good question. I think the second version is 'more definitive', if you can say such a thing. One of the reasons I redid it as more of a guitar version is because, over time, the first one started to feel a bit 'clunky', but although I say that, I wouldn't regard either version as absolutely definitive. It's a shame really that it's never been performed live really, but I doubt whether it ever will be. It would be quite a hefty undertaking for what, let's be honest, is a fairly minority audience! I'll say the second one, but it's personal taste between the two, I think.

Back to 1972, meanwhile, and another old college acquaintance of Hammill's re-entered the picture, with Gordian Troeller becoming his manager. Together they set up a company called Panel Enterprises to handle financial matters, which is worthy of note if only because of the rather wonderful disclaimer printed at the foot of their company stationery, which read – in the entirely 1970s anti-business spirit of the time – 'The ethos of this company is to do what has to be done in the best manner and with the least hassle possible, and to this end any offer contained herein does not constitute a contract'. This may be the only recorded instance of a contract explicitly stating that it is not worth the paper it is written on! Solicitors and lawyers reading this may well be going for a lie-down at this moment...

By November, he had the material ready for his next solo album, and in fact, premiered the songs at a show at the Marquee in London on 10 November, during which he was accompanied by David Jackson. The material was well received, but the album would not be recorded until the following year as he had another tour of – you guessed it – Italy, planned for December. He had been invited to appear as special guest on a short tour by Italian progressive rock band Le Orme, and as the Van der Graaf members were all admirers of the band, having played their music while touring the country themselves, he was delighted to accept. The two-week tour, which was another gruelling Italian schedule with double shows aplenty, was a success, with Le Orme being so impressed with Hammill that they went on to work together soon afterwards. Their most recent album, *Felona e Sorona* (the conceptual sci-fi story of two planets whose fates become tragically intertwined) had impressed Hammill when he heard them playing it at the shows, so he volunteered to write lyrics for it if they wanted to release an English version at any time. When the English recording was released (on Charisma) it met with variable reviews, including a hysterically scathing assassination in the *NME* by Ian McDonald, who described it as firstly 'absurdly ill-written and pretentious apologies for poems crooned by one of the dullest bunch of losers it's been my displeasure to encounter' before going on to label the release a 'blistering excrescence' and an 'aural pollutant', even managing to drag Emerson Lake and Palmer into his wild diatribe, referring to them (admittedly amusingly) as 'Cumbersome, Fake And Trauma'. Happily, not all reviews were quite so scathing, but such was often the lot of progressive rock bands at the hands of the *NME* in the 1970s!

So successful had the December 1972 tour been for Hammill, though, that he agreed to further such business early in the new year, but in a slightly different form...

1973 – Chameleons And Long Hellos

Chameleon In The Shadow Of The Night (Peter Hammill)

Personnel:

Peter Hammill: vocals, piano, acoustic and electric guitar, mellotron

David Jackson: saxophone, flute

Hugh Banton: organ, piano

Guy Evans: drums, percussion

Nic Potter: bass

Recorded at Sofa Sound and Rockfield Studios, February–March 1973

Produced by John Anthony

Released: May 1973 (Charisma)

Highest chart places: Did not chart

Running time: 50:21

All songs written by Peter Hammill

Tracklisting:

1. 'German Overalls' 7.04, 2. 'Slender Threads' 4.57, 3. 'Rock and Role' 6.41, 4. 'In The End' 7.21, 5. 'What's It Worth' 3.56, 6. 'Easy To Slip Away' 5.08, 7. 'Dropping The Torch' 4.11, 8. '(In The) Black Room / The Tower' 10.53

So 1973 began where 1972 had left off – with yet more live work in Italy! This time, however, it was a much briefer visit. Armando Gallo had been diligently trying to get Van der Graaf to reunite but had met with failure. What he could manage to do, however, was to get Peter Hammill and David Jackson together, which as 50 per cent of VdGG, he regarded as a lot better than nothing at all. The trip was less of a tour than a long weekend, consisting of just three days, over the weekend of 19–21 January. The trip was actually billed as 'The Charisma Festival', being another multi-band package from the label, and was regarded as a sort of moveable festival affair, touching down in three different places. There were four bands on the bill this time, with the old favourites of Genesis and Lindisfarne, together with new signings Capability Brown added to the line-up as opening act. Lindisfarne went on second, followed by Hammill / Jackson, with Genesis closing the shows. Lindisfarne were reportedly disappointed not to secure top billing, being flush with the big success they were enjoying in the UK at the time. The reality, however, was very different in Italy as, even going on after Capability Brown as third on the bill, they were met with audiences both unfamiliar with them and also unimpressed by their very 'English' folk-rock style, and they faced a hostile reaction and cries for Genesis and Hammill throughout their set. The fog on the Tiber was most assuredly not all theirs! In fact, so thrown off their game were they by this unexpected turn of events that they left the party after the first two shows and the final show in Rome featured only the other three bands. They didn't seem to be missed, as that final evening went down an absolute storm, playing to 12,000 fans.

The timing of the trip was both a bonus and a problem for David Jackson, as he had just got married, to Sue Cook, in a rather spur of the moment ceremony on 17 January. He left for Italy the following night, at 4 am, which must surely have made him extremely popular! However, the work was welcome as the couple were in need of the money. He does not have good memories of the trip, however, remembering himself and Peter, along with Gordian Troeller, driving all the way. Coming back, he recalls that they had to stay with friends of Gordian in Paris as they had run out of money and could not afford the ferry back over to England. Since this was, effectively, his honeymoon, it was far from ideal and must have contributed to his grim recollections of the trip.

Meanwhile, Peter Hammill was keeping very busy as, following solo shows in Bristol, Coventry and – bizarrely – Wilmslow (at the 'Grammar School For Boys', even more incongruously), late February saw recording begin on his solo album, to be entitled *Chameleon In The Shadow Of The Night*. Wanting to ensure that he would not be left isolated should record company support ever dry up (a very sensible precaution), he had installed a four-track TEAC recording system at his home in Sussex.

The bare bones of the less accompanied parts of the album with just Hammill himself playing were recorded first, on that set-up at his home. This rudimentary studio in his spare bedroom was christened 'Sofa Sound', though not because it had a sofa in there, or at least not directly. In fact, it was named after one of Hammill's several 'alter-ego' characters, a recording engineer named Rodney Sofa, under which guise he would be credited on the album itself. This skeletal structure comprised the basics of all but two of the album's eight songs and is responsible for the somewhat 'lo-fi' sound which the resulting album possesses. After this work was complete, he reconvened in Rockfield Studios in Wales, where his erstwhile VdGG colleagues (including Nic Potter) would accompany him. For this reason, together with some of the lyrical subject matter, and indeed one entire song, the album is inextricably bound up with the Van der Graaf Generator story, and many regard both this record and its successor the following year as almost 'unofficial Van der Graaf albums'.

The cover of the album was a striking one, again courtesy of Paul Whitehead, with the front bearing a photo of Hammill, from a short distance, sitting playing guitar on a lawn in front of a bush. This photo was in a circular frame, with Hammill's name in his own signature font above, and a large scorpion below it, as if carrying the circular photo. While it may seem odd that the scorpion is present while no chameleon appears anywhere, it is of course, a reference once again to Hammill's star sign of Scorpio. The rear cover has a strikingly other-worldly image of Hammill seated at a chessboard, which was produced by Whitehead photographing him and then painting the negative (if a colour photograph were taken of the rear cover, the negative would show up as a regular photo). The inner spread has a photo of Hammill standing in front of a rolling country landscape, with the lyrics printed behind. A couple of other things should be noted about the front cover. Firstly, in between his first and last name, is the first appearance of the strange logo which would go on to become synonymous with him throughout his career: it is, reportedly, made up of the letters in the word 'HAMMILL', together with the sign for Scorpio – though it is difficult to isolate all of those letters. Secondly, the scorpion on the cover was a real one, though not live. This fearsome-looking arachnid is a rare species known as the black scorpion, and had to be borrowed from, and returned to, the British Medical Association in order to be used – hence the cover credit to the BMA.

The album opens with two acoustic guitar-based songs. The first, 'German Overalls', is written in reference to the stressful nature of the band's tour of Germany in 1971, during which the front cover photo of Hammill and guitar was taken, in Hamburg on 20 May of that year. The odd title of the song has nothing to do with what workers in a Berlin factory might wear, as it is in fact, a punning reference to the anthem 'Deutschland Über Alles', which literally translates as Germany Over All. Banton and Jackson are namechecked in the lyric, and there are also in-joke references to 'Refugees' and 'Kosmos Tours'. This dramatic, seven-minute track comes with accompaniment by David Jackson and features some startlingly intense vocal cries, treated and phased. It's a statement of intent as an opener, without doubt. The following 'Slender Threads' is a trademark Hammill 'doomed relationship' song, driven by aching despair and bitterness, with just his voice and guitar taking on the delivery.

'Rock And Role', the third song, is different again, being a fairly straight-ahead, propulsive heavy rock song, with Hammill using his newly purchased Fender Stratocaster in a very upfront manner – his first recorded use of the electric guitar. Jackson, Evans and Potter are all on this one, giving it a band feel but in a very un-Van der Graaf way. Closing the first side is 'In The End', a song which depicts the ending of relationships and life events, clearly referencing the VdGG break-up on several occasions – the mention of 'no more travelling chess' for one being a giveaway. It's a superb song, and one of Hammill's finest lyrical works thus far. The accompaniment here is again Hammill alone, but this time on piano, and is the first real indication of just how remarkably intense his piano playing could be. He seems to hit the chords and notes in such a way as to transfer huge emotional weight into what he is singing, and when coupled with his formidably anguished vocal style, makes the song's impact enormous.

The second side begins with the acoustic guitar-based 'What's It Worth' (with Jackson again) which is almost the calm before the storm of the sublime 'Easy To Slip Away'. Again driven by Hammill's doom-laden piano chords (this time also with Potter and Jackson), the song is a sequel of sorts to 'Refugees', seeing the return of Mike and Susie, as Hammill sings of his having lost touch with them, lamenting the fact and how tragically easy it is to simply let relationships and friendships like that slip through your fingers as time passes almost unnoticed. With some mellotron also contributed by Hammill, it is a truly exceptional song, carrying so much obvious emotional power and genuine angst that, despite the personal subject matter, it cannot fail to strike a chord in any listener and bring to mind things that they themselves have allowed to 'slip away'.

'Dropping The Torch' is another guitar-based song which began as a poem, and is a depressingly claustrophobic piece with any hope or joy in life becoming progressively extinguished. Standard Hammill fare, then – but this really is the calm before the storm as it leads into the ten-minute epic, which is '(In The) Black Room / The Tower'. One of the songs intended for the planned VdGG album the previous year, and played by the band on stage in those final couple of months, this is where the lines between solo Hammill and full band Generator become inextricably blurred. Featuring the other three core musicians (no Potter on this one), it is a Van der Graaf piece in all but name, and still played by the band regularly almost 50 years later. The drama and intensity is a match for almost anything recorded by the band up to this point, with Hammill delivering a brilliant lyric relating to the apparent contradictions in life of fate versus free will, and rationale versus speculation. Tarot images abound, with The Tower being one of the cards in the deck, and also the Priestess, the Star and the Fool. There is also an interesting nod to Aldous Huxley's *Brave New World*, with one line talking of going to 'the feelies', which is the tactile equivalent of the cinema in Huxley's novel. It's a piece which finishes the album in spectacular style, and provided VdGG fans still distraught over the band's demise with a tangible life raft to cling on to. The CD reissue some decades later included a latterly unearthed track called 'Rain 3AM', another acoustic guitar-based song which uses the night-time and the gloomy weather to help conjure another litany of life's despair, and fits perfectly with the album. Live versions of 'Easy To Slip Away' and 'In The End' added to the same release are so frighteningly intense in their sparse and anguished delivery that one begins to fear that Hammill may collapse in emotional turmoil over his piano at any moment, unable to carry on. Essential for acolytes but certain to clear the room of the uninitiated, these were recorded five years later in 1978, in the All Souls Unitarian Church in Kansas, of all venues, and their slightly muddy sound is caused by them originating on a much-vaunted bootleg performance.

The album was released in May 1973 – obviously not troubling the chart compilers in very many places, but received enthusiastically by Van der Graaf aficionados. Directly following its release, Hammill was out on the road again, supporting Genesis at two shows in Paris and Brussels in early May. Following one more performance in Switzerland on 19 May (with no shows reported anywhere for over a week on either side of it, which seems logistically strange), he headed once again to Italy for ten shows in ten consecutive days – though mercifully this time only one per day! On the first two dates, in Rome and Bologna on the 27th and 28th, he was accompanied by Evans, Jackson and Banton in a full reunion of the classic VdGG line-up. Somewhat mischievously, though not entirely unexpectedly, the Italian promoters billed these shows as 'Van der Graaf Generator', which, while undoubtedly enticing in a healthy crowd, also led to unrest when they were confronted by a whole set of Hammill solo material, apart from 'Refugees' and 'Theme One' as encores. This was particularly problematic at the Bologna show, which saw a number of members of the ill-tempered crowd leaving during what was reportedly a rather rough-and-ready performance of 'Refugees'. The show in Rome saw the band joining Arthur Brown and his band Kingdom Come on the bill, along with the still relatively new Camel, who opened the show to very little appreciation. The show was hit by a delay, remembered as being due to a fire backstage, which apparently led to a lack of power, forcing the acts to choose between lights or amplification! There was an amusing incident (as there always seemed to be when Arthur was involved) recounted by Camel's drummer Andy Ward, as reported in *The Book*. The tale relates to Arthur's shoulder bag, which for some odd reason known only to himself, contained several pairs of underpants and a large jar of honey, and which was unfortunately run over by Gordian Troeller in his car. Ward remembers the bizarre sight of an enraged Arthur chasing after the car, waving some honey-soaked Y-fronts dramatically while swearing at the top of his voice.

The shows were very handy for David Jackson in particular, as he was already in Italy on a tour backing Anglo-Italian singer Alan Sorrenti, in a band which also included Francis Monkman from Curved Air (and later with Sky). Another interesting development arising from the show with Kingdom Come is that Guy Evans actually ended up joining the band as a result. They were using a drum machine for that show (their third and final album had been recorded without a drummer, using the drum machine exclusively – one of the first bands to use the technology in that way), and it seemed a perfect fit to have Guy provide 'real' drums again. He played two shows with them in London, including a high-profile one at the Rainbow Theatre, which was also notable for a bizarre guest appearance: as part of the show, a giant syringe appeared, with Arthur actually trapped within it, and on this occasion, reportedly David Bowie was in the syringe! Everything seemed to be going well but, with a combination of the Van der Graaf knack for the unexpected and the Arthur Brown travelling insanity circus, the band immediately split up, and Guy Evans' short-lived Kingdom Come tenure was in the past.

One thing that the Kingdom Come stint had given Guy was the impetus to start recording some music again, in particular with Banton and Jackson. The offers from Italy to do live work had come to nothing, but they still had music in them, which deserved to come out. And the unexpected catalyst which went some way to enabling that was the unexpected figure of all-too-brief Van der Graaf bassist Dave Anderson. Having left Hawkwind, he had designs on setting up a studio, and to that end, he bought a small derelict farm in Monmouth, Wales, which was in less than perfect repair, but would suit a studio in terms of layout quite nicely. Evans, who had remained in contact with him, approached him with a view to renting the place to do some recording, but there was the matter of studio equipment, which was difficult to rent in those days, being in quite short supply. So the pair decided to pool their collective resources and get the place kitted out, with Guy contacting people from a list of names which Anderson supplied to him, and they obtained just enough gear to function as an admittedly less-than-luxurious studio. Some Italian fans whom they had got to know had offered to back them with a recording project, so they were able to get started. David Jackson arrived first, but they found that some of the mismatched equipment wouldn't work together as it was, and they lacked the electronic or engineering know-how to overcome the issues. But they knew a man who could...

Enter, stage left, the 'Mad Professor' Hugh Banton. There was little which he would allow himself to be defeated by in terms of making repairs or improvements to electronic musical gear, and he wasn't about to start now. So he came down, bringing with him not only his expertise but also, with an eye on some productivity, his Hammond organ. The studio (which was christened Foel Studios, Welsh for 'treeless' or 'bare hill') was in a somewhat remote location, and certainly not in a state conducive to accommodation, but help was at hand in that regard, thanks to David Jackson's wife, Sue, who managed to secure the loan of a house, kindly granted by 'the parents of an ex-boyfriend'. It was a fascinating location, as the gentleman in question worked as a film producer, and the house – about 15 miles from the studio – was almost entirely furnished with props from movie sets.

After an abortive first day's attempted recording which was beset by equipment failures, Banton decided to work on the task alone to avoid distractions and get everything in running order. For a while, they hardly saw much of him, as he would disappear armed with manuals and soldering irons and such like. One particular night he had been away for a particularly long time, and Guy was becoming worried about what might have happened to him, so together with Sue Jackson, he headed over to see what was happening, at what was by now about 1 am. As they approached the studio building, they heard music emerging, and found it was Banton recording his umpteenth overdubbed keyboard part – he had decided to try recording something to test the equipment for its functionality, and got somewhat carried away, electing to work on a demo version of the 'Brain Seizure' piece, on which he played everything. From that point, the work began in earnest on what would eventually emerge as the album *The Long Hello*. The VdGG trio were augmented on the material by Nic Potter, and also two other musicians of their acquaintance – guitarist and bassist from Rare Bird, Ced Curtis, and also talented Italian guitarist Piero Messina, whom David Jackson had met while on tour over there. The material was all recorded quite quickly during August when they were defeated by the weather turning unseasonably wet. The road to the studio quickly became almost impossible to traverse with a large van, and a piano that had been hired for the work was rescued just before that vehicle became unable to be used. The music was all recorded, but the final mixing would have to wait as funds had become too tight at the time.

One man conspicuously absent from the sessions was Peter Hammill, though not from a lack of interest in the project. Rather, he deliberately absented himself as he recognised it was something they had to do, and that he would only be tempted to try to meddle in the proceedings. He did, however, give the project its name owing to the delay in its getting finished for release, as he suggested one day, 'It's taken so bloody long, why don't you call it *The Long Hello*?' – and a title was born.

****

Peter Hammill, meanwhile, was busying himself with his own recording issues. Keen to further test out his Sofa Sound set-up, he got back together once again with the recurring Judge Smith to collaborate on some demo recordings. Smith went to stay at Hammill's home for a while, and the pair put down versions of songs either written or co-written by Smith, such as 'Been Alone So Long' – which would go on to be recorded later by Hammill on his 1975 album *Nadir's Big Chance* – along with 'Time For A Change', 'Almost 23', 'Nineteen Nineteen', 'Sic Itur Ad Astra' (a quote from Virgil's *The Aeneid*, roughly translated as 'way to the stars'), along with the rather heroically titled 'Garibaldi Biscuits' and 'There's No Time Like The Present (Unless Perhaps It's Yesterday)'. Hammill did not do a whole lot of live shows around that precise time, but there was one notable appearance in Leeds on 22 June on the bill of an all-nighter which also starred Hawkwind, Caravan, Kingdom Come once again, and also Jack The Lad, who were a spin-off from Lindisfarne which included his old Six Bob Tour mates Rod Clements, Ray Laidlaw and Simon Cowe, and were actually making their debut on that occasion. They were a little more traditionally 'folk-rock' than Lindisfarne and were very good, though they never captured the public imagination with their four albums and split in 1976. Hammill did another John Peel session for Radio 1 on 24

July, performing 'Easy To Slip Away', 'German Overalls' and 'In The End', as well as Judge Smith's 'Time For A Change'. There was also another appearance on continental TV, performing 'German Overalls' and 'In The End' on the French show *Rock En Stock*.

In the second half of September, Hammill embarked on a short tour of the UK to promote *Chameleon In The Shadow Of The Night*, playing eight shows and including five tracks from the *Chameleon* album in the set, along with a couple from *Fool's Mate* and a few selections previewing his forthcoming, yet to be recorded album. For a show at the unlikely-sounding venue of Andover Boys Secondary School on the 20th, he was supported by The Judge Smith Effect, as demonstrated by an advertisement of the time, which described Hammill himself as 'Top Charisma Records star', which sounds slightly at odds with the gravitas of his performances!

Following the tour, it was straight into the studio to begin recording the next album. Once again, work began at Sofa Sound, with three tracks being recorded there ('Modern', 'Wilhelmena' and 'Rubicon'). One track, 'Red Shift' had already been recorded in April at Island Studios, featuring the guitar work of Randy California, the mercurial but brilliant guitarist with American band Spirit. Randy's penchant for being occasionally 'eccentric' was certainly not unknown, and such proved to be the case during the three days or so which he spent with the VdGG musicians in the studio. Partly because he arrived with his stepfather, Ed Cassidy, who also happened to be the drummer with Spirit, but more so because he apparently ate nothing but lemons – whole ones. Hammill remembers him walking round with a bag of them, and getting through a dozen or so straight from the bag. Guy Evans remembers the session: 'Yes, all of that is true. He insisted that Ed Cassidy auditioned me – he must have thought I was all right, because he let me play! The thing about the lemons is true as well. I don't know whether that's all he ate, but that's certainly all I ever saw him eat. He did just walk around with this bag full of lemons, that's correct.' In fact, the idea to record with California had first come up three years earlier when VdGG played with Spirit at the Lyceum in London, and Peter Hammill had been most impressed by him. The fact that it came to fruition was through a complete stroke of fortune (which seems to have been the theme of much of the Van der Graaf story at the time!), when the then-girlfriend of ex-band roadie Martin Pottinger, Christine Konczewski, who had moved into Guy Evans' flat with Pottinger at the time, turned out to be good friends with California since they had gone to high school together. Not a bad sort of coincidence considering the population of the United States to choose from, really.

The remaining three tracks on the forthcoming album (which would be released early the following year as *The Silent Corner And The Empty Stage*) were recorded at Rockfield with Jackson, Banton and Evans, while overdubs were also added to the Sofa Sound songs. Nic Potter does not appear on this one, as he had joined Rare Bird at this time for an album and the associated touring schedule.

Peter Hammill rounded off the year with a one-off show at London's Wigmore Hall on 27 October (the first non-classical concert ever to be staged at the prestigious venue) followed by another series of shows in mainland Europe. A short run of gigs in Belgium, France and Switzerland in the latter half of November was followed by another packed Italian visit, with 14 shows in two weeks between the 2nd and 15th of December. There was no accompaniment at these performances, which featured Hammill alone on either guitar or piano for various songs, and reviews were generally extremely positive.

Guy Evans, meanwhile, was taking part in another – albeit fairly brief – musical venture of his own. Having moved to Cornwall in order to decompress a little from the capital and clear his head somewhat, he fell in with a group by the unlikely name of Charlie and the Wideboys, who had been looking for a drummer. Mostly living an unconventional yet, as Guy has described it, 'fairly idyllic' lifestyle in some ruined cottages on the coast, the band were a sort of 'pub-rock', straight rock-and-roll band as far removed from the world of Van der Graaf Generator as it was possible to get. They were a fairly successful live act, heading to London once a week for a residency at the Marquee, and released an EP during Guy's tenure with them, featuring four tracks, including the lead-off and featured cut 'Gilly I Do'. Though Guy was with them for a relatively short time, the band were still active until 2020, when band leader and frontman Charlie Ainley sadly passed away.

However, 1974 would see a very busy year for Peter Hammill in particular, with two solo albums being released, but would also prove to be a significant year for each of the Van der Graaf quartet in different ways.

1974 – A Silent Stage Is Not A Home

The Silent Corner and the Empty Stage (Peter Hammill)
Personnel:

Peter Hammill: vocals, guitar, piano, mellotron, harmonium, bass guitar, oscillator

Hugh Banton: organ, bass pedals, bass guitar, backing vocals

Guy Evans: drums, percussion

David Jackson: alto, tenor and soprano saxophones, flute

Randy California: lead guitar on 'Red Shift'

Recorded at Sofa Sound, Sussex and Rockfield Studios, Monmouth, September and October 1973

'Red Shift' recorded at Island Studios, London, April 1973

Produced by John Anthony and Peter Hammill

Release date: 8 February 1974 (Charisma)

All songs by Peter Hammill

Tracklisting:

1. 'Modern' 7.28, 2. 'Wilhelmina' 5.18, 3. 'The Lie (Bernini's Saint Theresa)' 5.41, 4. 'Forsaken Gardens' 6.16, 5. 'Red Shift' 8.11, 6. 'Rubicon' 4.41, 7. 'A Louse Is Not A Home' 12.47

In Camera (Peter Hammill)
Personnel:

Peter Hammill: vocals, guitar, piano, mellotron, harmonium, bass guitar, synthesizer

Guy Evans: drums

Chris Judge Smith: backing vocals, percussion

Paul Whitehead: percussion

David Hentschel: ARP programming

Recorded at Sofa Sound, Sussex and Trident Studios, London, December 1973–April 1974

Produced by Peter Hammill

Release date: July 1974 (Charisma)

All songs by Peter Hammill

Tracklisting:

1. 'Ferret And Featherbird' 3.43, 2. '(No More) The Sub-mariner' 5.47, 3. 'Tapeworm' 4.20, 4. 'Again' 3.44, 5. 'Faint-Heart And The Sermon' 6.42, 6. 'The Comet, The Course, The Tail' 6.00, 7. 'Gog' 7.40, 8. 'Magog (In Bromine Chambers)' 9.41

The Long Hello

Personnel:

David Jackson: saxophone, flute, piano

Hugh Banton: all instruments on 'Brain Seizure', bass on 'The O Flat Session'

Guy Evans: drums

Nic Potter: bass

Piero Messina: electric guitar, acoustic guitar, piano

Ced Curtis: electric guitar, bass on 'Fairhazel Gardens'

Recorded at Foel Studio, August 1973

Produced by Guy Evans

Release Date: 1974 (Italy, United Artists), 1976 (UK, self-released)

Tracklisting:

1. 'The Theme From (Plunge)' (Jackson) 5.31, 2. 'The O Flat Session' (Messina) 5.32, 3. 'Morris To Cape Roth' (Jackson) 6.33, 4. 'Brain Seizure' (Banton) 4.01, 5. 'Fairhazel Gardens' (Jackson, Messina) 7.56, 6. 'Looking At You' (Jackson) 6.16, 7. 'I Lost My Cat' (Jackson) 8.28

Peter Hammill's *The Silent Corner And The Empty Stage*, recorded the previous autumn, was finally released on 8 February 1974. Containing three tracks which could, to various degrees, be described as full band affairs, the record was a big step forward from *Chameleon* in terms of its polish and overall sound, and also arguably in terms of material as well, despite the excellence of that previous album. Certainly, in a poll to find the favourite Hammill solo album among fans, *Silent Corner* came out top by a significant margin, while 'A Louse Is Not A Home' topped the votes for best individual track from his catalogue, so the album's high regard among the fan base is indisputable.

Just three of the seven tracks this time out contain only Hammill on the recordings, and two of them open the album in quick succession. 'Modern' is a dramatic opener, spiky and impassioned, and has remained a feature of many solo shows even to this day, while 'Wilhelmena' is a much gentler song, with Hammill crooning it quite movingly to the accompaniment of his own acoustic guitar and piano (he also plays bass himself on these opening tracks). The song was written for Guy Evans' newly born daughter, expressing his hope that she may grow up happily in a flawed world; this may seem odd, since the baby was named Tamra, but the truth is, as Guy has said in *The Book*, 'She didn't have a name for a while, and we used to call her 'Willy'!' Indeed, in the song, the name Wilhelmena is never used, and it only references the name Willy.

From this point on, however, the album goes up a significant notch, with 'The Lie (Bernini's Saint Theresa)' being one of Peter's most powerful songs, both lyrically and musically. Featuring mainly Hammill, with accompaniment only from Hugh Banton, the song takes aim in coruscating fashion at the Roman Catholic environment Peter Hammill had grown up and gone to school in, his voice pushed to its limits as he slices through the subject matter in syllables of red-hot steel, his voice further enhanced by howlingly distorted treatment at key points. The inspiration for the track was a statue in Rome (referenced, though misspelt, in the subtitle of the song) by the Italian sculptor Gian Lorenzo Bernini, with the full name of *Ecstasy of St Teresa*. Certainly an unconventional and potentially divisive statue in itself, it represents a moment described by Teresa herself when she was pierced in the chest by a flaming arrow wielded by an angel, causing both 'pain and rapture'. This image both piqued Hammill's interest and inspired memories of his childhood relationship with the Church, as he later explained in an interview with *ZigZag* magazine:

In my adolescence, I was very into religion at one point, but I got into it from the point of view of being in love with all the female saints. It was a great confusion of sex and religion, which is what the song is about… [I believe that] behind the panoplies of religion – not just Christianity, but because I was brought up a Catholic that's the one I know and write about – there is truth, but the truth is completely masked in all the outward pomp and circumstance… 'The Lie' is the religion in the way it is presented to you, because it does hide the truth, and I believe the saints got to the truth, but they certainly didn't get to it by going to Mass every morning and benediction in the evening – that wasn't the truth, which is how it was presented to you at school.

Following on from this is the sublime 'Forsaken Gardens', which finishes the first side of the record in a way which is both serenely beautiful and achingly sorrowful, in a way that few can pull off quite as completely as Hammill. All three of his erstwhile bandmates accompany him on this masterpiece.

The aforementioned 'Red Shift', featuring Randy California's pulsating lead guitar throughout, opens the second side in a way which sounds scarcely like anything else in the Hammill catalogue – the combination of the lyric, California's guitar and the echoed, other-worldly vocal treatment making this sound even more rooted in science fiction (or rather simply 'science', perhaps) than even 'Pioneers Over c' had been. It's a superb piece, spread languorously over its eight minutes before giving way to the much more stripped-back 'Rubicon' with Hammill alone once more. All of this is leading up to what is in many ways the main event, however, 'A Louse Is Not A Home', a complex picture of a descent into madness, insecurity and psychosis delivered in brilliantly allegorical 'house' imagery. As with 'Black Room', this had been intended as a Van der Graaf track and had been played on stage in 1972, and closes an album which is as close as fans could have got to seeing what a new VdGG album might have sounded like in 1974. And it sounded exceptionally good.

The cover, this time out, dispenses with Paul Whitehead's work, as he had by this time moved to the USA, and instead is designed by Bettina Hohls, who had taken the front cover photograph for the *Chameleon* album. The Hammill logo is again present in the bottom left, while Hammill's head appears on the back, in the form of a drawing which is in fact, taken directly from a photo he posed for in a park, with what looks like a pair of spectacles around his neck indeed being just that in the photograph. The rest of the design is very abstract (featuring the title and Hammill's name in his own handwriting), but is strikingly effective – far more so than the inner gatefold, which is certainly striking but far less impressive in terms of communicating the contents within. The inner sleeve has detailed notes together with all of the lyrics – this time all painstakingly written out in Peter's own hand. Several surreal characters appear in the credits once again – Rodney Sofa is back, credited with 'incidental intrusions', together with Lizard Bizarre and The Dazzler. The former is apparently a reference to John Anthony, while The Dazzler is shortform for The Derby Dazzler, a pseudonym characterisation used by Hammill when taking part in the VdGG sporting events. Indeed, three of these intriguing inventions are credited herein, namely 'tap-bat', 'picture darts' and 'golfwinks'. It is also notable as the first occurrence of David Jackson being credited with his nickname of 'Jaxon'.

The album was quite well received by many of the critics, but what few could have known was that the hyper-creative Hammill was already midway through creating the follow-up, recorded between the tail end of December and April, but largely during January and February. It would be released in July, only five months after *Silent Corner*, and entitled *In Camera*. The recording sessions would be accompanied by some unwelcome drama and near-tragedy, however, as right at the beginning of recording (in the Sofa Sound home studio), Peter's brother Andrew, a student at the University of Sussex, was knocked off his bike by a lorry and was in a coma for some time, remaining in hospital throughout the recording. Happily, he recovered, but he was in intensive care for at least a week, and Peter has said that going out to see him was virtually the only time he left the studio during those early stages of the recording.

Also happening in this early part of 1974 was the publication of Peter Hammill's book, *Killers, Angels, Refugees*, through Charisma Books, which included all lyrics to date, some short stories and also some explanatory notes about some songs. When talking about the book in interviews, he was to claim that he had a follow-up due to appear the following year, which would this time concentrate on the short stories (15 of them). Unfortunately, the collapse of Charisma Books as a publishing business meant that this project was shelved, and when the book did eventually appear some years later under the title *Mirrors, Dreams, Miracles*, it was largely made up of lyrics, with the short story element severely curtailed.

Hammill had done a couple of UK shows in early April towards the end of the *In Camera* work – including one in a church in Kingston, London, which notably featured Hugh Banton again, playing the church organ. Interestingly, the first the audience knew of Hugh's involvement at this event, according to reports from Peter at the time, was midway through the show when, hidden from view until that point from the audience in the pews, he began playing the organ as Hammill paused playing himself ('a good moment', as he recalled it). Nevertheless, live appearances were very few and far between in the first third of the year until, immediately following the recording of the album, Hammill left for Canada for a short tour as support to Genesis in April, who were midway through a full North American tour. Remaining in Montreal following two Genesis shows there, on 20/21 April, Hammill played a solo show in the city on the 24th, continuing his unusual habit of performing in schools – this time at a high school called Cegep Maisonneuve. While on that Canadian sojourn, he was confronted by an extraordinary number of people asking him about Van der Graaf Generator, which actually served to pique his interest as regards playing with the band again. As he said to *Melody Maker* on his return: 'I came back and I began to think, well, it's all very well going out with a guitar and a piano and doing the complete soul exposition, but there are other things lacking.' All of which suggests that we may have had the Canadian fan base playing an unexpectedly significant part in the eventual decision to re-form. Five solo shows followed in May and early

June – one each in Paris and Switzerland, and three more in the ongoing trawl around the educational establishments of the world, with UK shows at Thames Polytechnic, Sheffield University and Judge Smith's old seat of learning, Oundle School (the 'Oundle School Folk Club', which certainly doesn't sound like a regular stop on the UK touring circuit). The Thames Polytechnic show was on a Friday, and not a 'school night' – which was just as well as Hammill reportedly showed up somewhat late for it, eventually taking the stage at midnight! Clearly, no music curfews in force there…

Following this, *In Camera* gained its release in July. The record this time out was a much more stripped-back affair, with no full band epics and only Guy Evans from the band appearing (and even then on only two out of eight tracks). Judge Smith also makes another return to the story, contributing backing vocals and percussion. This is not to say that the album is in any way lacking in power and gravitas – on the contrary, it is a highly potent release, with Hammill himself overdubbing on, variously, guitar, piano, mellotron, bass guitar, synthesizer and even harmonium – essentially, everything except percussion. On this album, if you didn't hit it, Hammill played it.

Some familiar themes are mined lyrically, with 'Faint-Heart And The Sermon' being another obvious reference to his religious upbringing, while the nostalgic '(No More) The Sub-mariner' takes its title in wryly punning style from the Marvel comic-book character 'Namor The Sub-mariner'. 'Ferret And Featherbird' is a song which was originally recorded way back in 1969, prior to *The Aerosol Grey Machine*, but never released, and is a perfect fit here, while 'Tapeworm' hits a far more aggressive tone to give the first side of the album some greater contrast. The real heavy-duty stuff comes on the second side, however, which sees the opening track 'The Comet, The Course, The Tail' take inspiration from the comet Kohoutek, and somehow extrapolate it into a weighty musing on the compatibility between established social order and individual free will. It's a great song, but using the word 'weighty' here must be used with caution and in a relative way, as the remainder of the album is taken up by the fearsome 17-minute barrage which is the two-part 'Gog' / 'Magog (In Bromine Chambers)'.

'Gog', lasting for around eight of those minutes, is an astonishing piece. The lyric, taking the rough template of the Rolling Stones' 'Sympathy For The Devil' as its starting point and proceeding to race away with it towards the horizon, is brutally harsh, uncompromising, thought-

provoking and nothing short of brilliantly erudite. The subject of the song is far from the simple 'Lucifer' creation that the admittedly brilliant Jagger lyric conjures up, being altogether more abstract, thoughtful and darkly arcane. 'My soul is cast in crystal /
Yet unrevealed beneath the knife', offers a terrifyingly intense Hammill. 'Some see me shining, others have me dull / Gun-metal and cut diamond – I am ALL / Some swear they see me weeping in the poppy fields of France – In the tumbling of the dice see them fall!' Musically and lyrically, it is one of the most startlingly intense things that either Hammill solo or VdGG as an entity have ever committed to tape. Yet even this is easy listening compared to the sonic barrage which is 'Magog (In Bromine Chambers)', being around nine minutes of what he has described as *musique concrete*, and conjuring up a sense of profound unease and dread. *Musique concrete* is defined as 'utilising recorded sounds as raw material... often modified through the application of audio signal processing and tape music techniques... assembled into a form of montage'. It is similar in a way to The Beatles' 'Revolution 9', and certainly as divisive among fans. There are two 'verses' of spoken words seemingly referring to a less than angelic afterlife, and this is almost certainly the significance of the 'bromine chambers'. It is among the most far-out into the hinterlands of musical experimentation that Peter Hammill would ever go, and it is not recommended to listen to alone in the dark, or strange things and imaginings may creep up on the unsuspecting brain. And no, the album did not make the charts!

The cover on this occasion was much simpler – and, it must be said, far less impressive. Hammill poses on the front in a cape dramatically and flamboyantly donned, like a sort of glam-rock vampire, while the rear cover (no gatefold this time) has a similar photo, which on some editions is in monochrome. The album did come with a lyric sheet within, including photos which oddly dated from 1969, but it is still a rather basic and uninvolving package. It is, notably, and appropriately, dedicated to Andrew Hammill, Peter's brother. Note that the phrase 'in camera' refers to something taking place in private, or behind closed doors – and specifically, in a legal sense, in a judge's chambers. The album being mainly recorded alone, shut away in the Sofa Studio room, probably has a bearing on the title.

While all of this was going on, the other VdGG men had somewhat scattered to the four winds, with very different projects going on. David Jackson had been forced by mid-1974 through financial necessity to (temporarily) quit the music business full-time and find gainful employment in the world outside – in this case, working as a van driver for a paper manufacturing company, delivering in and around London. While doing this job (which he has said he actually enjoyed as he had always loved driving vans), he took the opportunity to get a significant amount of dental work done, to 'completely rebuild' his teeth ('saxophone playing is very heavy on teeth', as he has remarked). Nic Potter, conversely, was still very much active musically, notably forming a working partnership with ex-Free guitarist Paul Kossoff, with whom he had actually been in the same class at school – a fact which Kossoff had forgotten, but Potter had not, reminding him of it the first time they spoke. The pair spent some months rehearsing together as a trio together with former Spooky Tooth drummer Mike Kellie, but frustratingly never got as far as recording any music or playing live shows, so we can only surmise as to their output.

Hugh Banton had also been rather busy, very much on the musical front, as he had finally retrieved his Hammond organ from the crumbling farmhouse which was Foel Studios, where it had remained since the *Long Hello* sessions the previous year. The wooden casing was coming apart by now from years of use and carrying in and out of venues, so he took the only practical decision which was to dismantle it and extricate it from the building in pieces. This would go on to have a significant follow-on, as it provided the catalyst for the major organ building and customisation project, which he christened 'HB1', and would take a long time to eventual completion. He began plans for this in Torquay, where he was living at that time, but soon moved it to London – firstly to Chalk Farm Studios, opposite the famous Roundhouse venue, where he had arranged with Charisma to record some of his material in demo form, aided by Jackson and Evans. Not a tremendous amount of significance emerged from the sessions, but it was notable for the fact that Sue Lowe was working as a tape-op at the studio. Hugh, moving back to London, needed somewhere to live and moved into a flat with Sue and Chalk Farm sound engineer Neil Richmond. Hugh and Sue soon became an item at this point and would marry the following year. HB1 would accompany him to the capital, and become ensconced upstairs in the studio for a while, where Hugh would continue to work on it.

Around this time he had also accepted an offer to join a band called Seventh Wave, which unusually featured no fewer than three keyboard players. The core duo of Ken Elliott and Kieran O'Connor had released an album under the Seventh Wave name, and had put a new seven-piece line-up (or eight, nine or ten, depending upon who was credited as a member) together for live work. Neil Richmond, who had produced the first album, was recruited on 'offstage electronic effects and tape loops' for that expanded live ensemble, all of whom would contribute to the follow-up, titled *Psi-Fi*.

By this time well ensconced in the Chalk Farm studio, having been doing work as a studio session synthesizer programmer, among other things, it proved to be the ideal location to finally finish up the mixing of the *Long Hello* album, which had lain idle since the previous year's recordings had concluded. In August, he and Guy Evans reconvened to finish things up, with the original tapes still in Guy's possession, No extra actual recording was done, but the final mixing did throw up some interesting challenges, as Guy remembers now:

> The album still stands up pretty well, I think. It did throw up some interesting anomalies and challenges in the mixing of it, mainly to do with the technical limitations of the time. For instance, the overdubs on the track 'I Lost My Cat'. Dave wanted to do all those flowing flute lines, and we just didn't have enough tracks to do it, so we did a little working mix of the backing track, which was drums, bass and piano, and put that on to one track of a new reel of eight-track tape. Then we recorded all of the flute parts on the remaining seven tracks and then mixed those down to stereo on a separate Revox tape machine, and then 'flew' that stereo flute mix back onto the backing track by hand, speeding up and slowing down the tape by hand to keep them matching up. It worked because it's such a dreamy sort of piece – it wouldn't have been possible to do that if it had been more rhythmically precise.

The album was finally released later in the year, though initially only in Italy, appearing in a cover design which featured an oddly fantasy-tinged landscape, somewhat reminiscent of a more colourful variant of Caravan's *In The Land Of Grey And Pink*. The album was eventually released in the UK in 1976 as a private pressing of 5,000, each individually numbered with a stamp on the rear cover, in a much sparser monochrome line-drawn cover design. Track titles tended towards the surreal, such as David Jackson's aforementioned 'I Lost My Cat', 'Morris To Cape Roth' and 'The Theme From (Plunge)'. One track, Piero Messina's 'The O Flat Session' can be explained by the fact that the imaginary note of O flat would be written Ob, which would make the title 'The Obsession', while Jackson's 'Fairhazel Gardens' takes its name from the location in London where he had been living with his wife, Sue. It is odd that the more ornate Italian design was not retained for the UK release, as it is certainly the superior cover, though the individual numbering is a nice touch (mine is number 800!)

Back in Peter Hammill Land, things started to happen after the release of *In Camera*, albeit slowly. Two more radio appearances were recorded in August and September, being another John Peel session (performing 'Faint-Heart And The Sermon', '(No More) The Sub-mariner' and, bizarrely, 'The Emperor In His War Room') followed by an interview for Capital Radio in late September during which Peter talked about his plans and also played a song live, which again was the somewhat unexpected 'Black Room'. Two upcoming shows were alluded to in that interview, being appearances in November at the Wigmore Hall – notable for the fact that Evans, Banton and Jackson all accompanied him for the first time since those incorrectly listed shows that had taken place in Italy. What he failed to do during that interview was to make any mention of the fact that, around a month beforehand – following a trip to Germany to see Bettina and Klaus Hohls – he had made the decision that it was time to re-form the band. He asked Hugh Banton first, who agreed straight away despite feeling a little bad about letting down Seventh Wave, with whom he had nearly finished recording their second album *Psi-Fi*. Following that, they sounded out the other two, who both agreed to park the other projects they were working on. Jackson had nothing too pressing – having retired from the business full-time, he had spent some time jamming and rehearsing material with ex-Atomic Rooster man Nick Graham (their wives were friends as it happens) with a view to a band called Juggernaut, but appropriately, given the name, it never got on the road. Guy Evans was still with Charlie And The Wideboys (just) at the time, but he was happy to break away from them, as they had gained a contract with Anchor Records which entailed them leaving the idyllic Cornish location and becoming based in London again – something he wasn't keen on doing, particularly since the move away from the capital had been one of the main reasons for his joining up with the band in the first place.

By the time of those November shows, the foursome knew exactly what was going to be happening, and rehearsals for the returning VdGG were started in December. The rest of the world, and even the band's fan base, would have to wait six months or so before finding out this exciting news.

First up, however, would be yet another Hammill solo album, this time with all of the other three playing on it, in something which could be seen as a sort of 'dress rehearsal' for the return of Van der Graaf...

1975 – The Undercover Men

Nadir's Big Chance (Peter Hammill)

Personnel:

Peter Hammill: vocals, electric and acoustic guitars, piano, clavinet, harmonium, bass guitar

Hugh Banton: organ, piano, bass guitar

Guy Evans: drums, percussion

David Jackson: saxophone

Recorded at Trident Studios, London and Rockfield Studios, Monmouth, December 1974

Produced by Peter Hammill

Release date: 1 February 1975 (Charisma)

Highest chart places: Did not chart

Running Time: 48:24

Tracklisting:

1. 'Nadir's Big Chance' (Hammill) 3.27, 2. 'The Institute Of Mental Health, Burning' (Hammill, Smith) 3.50, 3. 'Open Your Eyes' (Hammill) 5.10, 4. 'Nobody's Business' (Hammill) 4.15, 5. 'Been Alone So Long' (Smith) 4.20, 6. 'Pompeii' (Hammill) 4.50, 7. 'Shingle Song' (Hammill) 4.10, 8. 'Airport' (Hammill) 3.02, 9. 'People You Were Going To' (Hammill) 5.10, 10. 'Birthday Special' (Hammill) 3.40, 11. 'Two Or Three Spectres' (Hammill) 6.20

Godbluff

Personnel:

Peter Hammill: vocals, piano, clavinet, electric guitar

David Jackson: saxophone, flute

Hugh Banton: organ, bass pedals, bass guitar

Guy Evans: drums and percussion

Recorded at Rockfield Studios, June 1975

Produced by Van der Graaf Generator

Released: 10 October 1975 (UK: Charisma, US: Mercury)

Highest chart places: Did not chart

Running time: 37:44

Tracklisting:

1. 'The Undercover Man' (Hammill) 7.32, 2. 'Scorched Earth' (Hammill, Jackson) 9.44, 3. 'Arrow' (Hammill, Banton, Evans, Jackson) 9.48, 4. The Sleepwalkers (Hammill) 10.40

Come the dawn of 1975, the four members of Van der Graaf Generator were officially together again – or perhaps that should be 'unofficially', as the world at large were not going to be let into the secret for some time yet. The first activity for the year was the release of the Hammill solo album on which they had all contributed, and on this occasion, it was a rather different offering to *In Camera* – or indeed, either of the two preceding ones. It could be said to have more in common with *Fool's Mate*, but even then, only in terms of the more concise songs (and more of them) rather than the actual sound of the record.

The album title was *Nadir's Big Chance*, coming from the fact that the concept of the record was that it was allowing Peter's 'alter-ego' Ricky Nadir to take over and have his way with the material. In a startlingly prescient manner for early 1975, Ricky Nadir was, effectively, a punk. He wielded an ice-blue Stratocaster (Hammill's own latest acquisition), and specialised in short, sharp, direct songs laden with attitude and swagger – at least, for the most part, anyway. The album consisted of 11 tracks, of which only two reached the five-minute mark, with much of the material being defiantly guitar-driven rock. The title track, in particular, is punk before the template had even been properly drawn up, and rails against the music business in its upfront and confrontational lyrical content. I think it's fair to say that lines such as 'If the guitars don't get you, the drums will' is quite a departure from 'Easy To Slip Away', ' Forsaken Gardens' or 'A Louse Is Not A Home'.

Several other songs (such as the single 'Birthday Special') continued that proto-punk energy, but there are also delicate ballads (albeit concise ones) to provide the balance. 'Shingle Song' in particular, is one of Hammill's finest short pieces, but there are even a couple of trips back to the archives for unexpected additions. The quickly withdrawn 1969 single 'People You Were Going To' gets a resurrection here, which would have surely amazed people, had they realised that it had even existed back then, which relatively few at the time would have. Judge Smith's song 'Been Alone So Long' is another which we would not have put bets on Peter turning his hand to, but he does so in a brilliantly expressive and fragile manner which teases the very best out of the piece. Another Smith contribution – this time a co-write with Hammill – is the dramatic and intense 'The Institute Of Mental Health, Burning', which so impressed the young John Lydon / Johnny Rotten that when he appeared on the radio in his Sex Pistols guise, he waxed lyrical about his admiration for Peter Hammill in general, and actually played that song to illustrate his praise.

If that surprises some, however, it actually shouldn't – as Van der Graaf
were always the one 'prog' band above all others who were respected by
the more discerning punk listeners, as they always possessed an abrasive
attitude and anarchistic musical bent which set them apart from their
more mellifluously symphonic brethren, should we say. Let's face it, you
couldn't get more 'punk' in spirit than Peter Hammill howling his lyrics
like a soul in torment while a manic-looking figure in a leather hat played
two massively overdriven and distorted electric saxophones at the same
time. 'Shine On You Crazy Diamond' or 'Close To The Edge', this was not.

The album came in a package which reflected the concept and contents,
with a front cover design made up of a series of monochrome 'contact'
photo prints. The back cover featured some handwritten notes by Peter
himself about the album, explaining the whole concept and idea of
'Nadir' himself, together with the track listing and credits and a blurry
photo of the man himself. It's all monochrome, in white on black, and
the overall effect, while it does undeniably fit in with the concept of the
record, is a little underwhelming. Of course, that was intentionally so, and
thus it's hard to complain about!

As soon as the album was released, the band decamped to a building in
Hertfordshire called Norton Canon Rectory, with a view to rehearsing and
preparing for their big return. Or at least, three of them did. Hugh Banton
remained behind in London with the unwieldy carcass of the HB1 organ
project, still frantically working on it whenever the time permitted – which
was a lot of it. He had moved the instrument-in-progress out of Chalk Farm
Studios a couple of weeks earlier, after giving his notice to leave Seventh
Wave, but he had managed to secure a new base of operations for his
work. Guy had been going out with an actress named Gennie Nevinson,
and as fortune would have it, her mother had a spare room in her house
near Hampstead Heath, and Hugh was able to move HB1 in there lock,
stock and bass pedals, so to speak. In fact, he had already done some
design work there with David Jackson on the latter's sax set-up, so the
timing was rather convenient. He worked there on the organ for a short
while, before Peter Hammill and Gordian Troeller paid him a visit on 26
February, asking whether he could join them at Norton Canon. They were
finding that rehearsals without such a critical element of the band's sound
was proving difficult and frustrating, and so they persuaded Hugh to move
the great organ carcass once again, over to Norton Canon where a spare
room was available for him to continue the construction work, while also
allowing some full band rehearsals to take place.

As it happened, this relocation proved only partially successful at first since, while some full band rehearsals did take place, most of Hugh's time was spent tinkering 'under the hood' as it were on the still-not-complete HB1, in its new lair in a spare room of the rectory. Eventually, at the beginning of April, when it became clear that no end was in imminent sight to the construction work, a Hammond C3 was rented for the purpose of continuing the rehearsals full-time and uninterrupted. At the same time, David Jackson had been doing his own crazy construction project as, along with John Goodman, he produced two odd creations nicknamed 'the Creda' and 'the Rizla'. The Creda was so named because of the inspiration Jackson took from his oven, near which he was working, with this black steel construction containing 'the rings' (a Gibson Maestro with octaves up and down, tone controls and mighty distortion, all operated by a foot controller), 'the grill' (a Copycat Echo tape loop), and 'the oven' (a combination power supply and pre-amp, designed by Hugh and christened MR2, or Mad Robert Two). The Rizla, meanwhile, was a rectangular steel case housing pedals and the like, which was so named because it was the same shape as a giant Rizla cigarette paper packet, and also the exact height of said packet stood on its end. This behemoth housed an array including foot switches, volume and echo pedals using a light-sensoring device, wah-wah and chorus pedals, and finally, three brass organ pistons. Jackson explained in the later compilation *The Box* that these pistons were intended for some upcoming technological breakthrough which never quite arrived and ended up being used as 'rather therapeutic springy foot-rests, often misinterpreted as stunning footwork by fans!'

To make things even more impressive, this entire array of technical wizardry was cabled together and could be controlled from Jackson's 'utility belt', which contained a routing box and several switches, one of which was operated by his elbow. With this battery of effects at his beck and call, and a long belt lead in place, he could stalk the stage while not only playing two saxophones in a holder at the same time, but also controlling them in a way not unlike manhandling a set of belt-housed bagpipes. As far as the traditional 'horn section' went, Van der Graaf Generator were most assuredly not even in the vicinity of Kansas anymore.

One thing which was in plentiful supply during these sessions was new material to work on, as Peter Hammill had been astonishingly prolific over the previous six months since the decision to re-form. According to his recollection, the composition of three out of four of the *Godbluff* songs were finished prior to rehearsals (only 'The Undercover Man' had yet to be completed), as well as the whole of the *Still Life* album and 'Masks' from the following *World Record*. It is believed that the song 'Urban', which only ever surfaced on the *Vital* live recording, was also written at this time. The Banton-less trio recorded a further two tracks, which would only appear in the following decade on the odds-and-sods compilation *Time Vaults*, these being 'Rift Valley' and 'Coil Night'. Gordian Troeller was doubling up his management duties with those of head chef at the time, as he took his mission to keep the band fed seriously – to the extent that, planning ahead in terms of meat supplies, he bought a cow. A whole one. It was stored at the local butcher's (in his freezer, we assume, rather than roaming the shop!), until some part of it was ready for consumption, at which point Gordian the Masterchef would collect the cut in question. He also bought a number of pigeons and a hare at a local pub one day, so there was a varied diet on offer at least!

On the business side of things, the band realised that they had to steer clear of the trap of any management affairs being handled by the record company again, after the Charisma management of the earlier incarnation proved to be less than ideal. To this end, they set up a company called Static Enterprises to handle all of that. Gordian Troeller was made an equal partner in the company, with a five-way split (to give him 'added incentive', as David Jackson put it), but things did retain a little of the old quirkiness with the company stationery featuring a small, and rather charming, cartoon drawing of the four musicians at work just above the list of directors! As Guy Evans recalls of that process now:

> We were pretty excited about being back, and we were firing on all four cylinders as far as the music went, but we had to get the business side right. We went with Charisma as the record company again, but we didn't want them managing us again as well – it's a very good idea to keep those things separate. We'd built up a sort of amorphous debt over the years, which it was quite difficult to find out exact details about as to what it was made up of. We had to repay that, so we set up a situation we could control, with a manager in place whom we had chosen and had faith in, and a company set up to look after things. We also had a deal with Charisma that we could at least work with – it was a bit of a tussle between 'yes, they do need to be paid back' but also 'we need enough cash to operate'. It was quite exciting having that set-up, we had our own

offices in Portobello Road, and we were able to make decisions about what tours we would do and so on.

The news of the band's reunion was also finally officially disseminated at this point, with Gordian sending out a newsletter of sorts to fans, containing the announcement as well as touring and recording plans.

****

As April drew to a close, work was brought to a halt for a short while again, but on this occasion, for a planned endeavour: Hugh Banton was getting married to Sue on the 25th (also his birthday, of which she has said – quite wisely – that it would provide a 'good prompt for remembering anniversaries'). They were married in Sale Town Hall, Cheshire, quite near to Timperley where Sue's parents lived. A quick weekend's honeymoon preceded a move back to London and their home in Cricklewood, on the rather splendidly named Shoot Up Hill, before the band also returned from Norton Canon, and work recommenced in earnest. Needing to do some rehearsing in what simulated an actual stage environment, they had four days booked at the start of May at Shepperton Studios, an old film studio which Led Zeppelin had used to film some fill-in 'concert' footage for their film *The Song Remains The Same* and where The Who would go on to film some live material for their own movie *The Kids Are Alright*. Tony Stratton-Smith even dropped by during the time at Shepperton, at the same time that Geoff Barton was reporting on proceedings for *Sounds*, and Strat provided Barton with the rather wonderful quote that 'Time has proved the lasting quality of Van der Graaf Generator's work, and in my opinion, the lay-off was necessary to let the rest of the world catch up.' Quite, sir!

Once this stage practice had been undertaken, the next logical step was a little actual low-key live work to get the feel of an audience situation again, and Wales was chosen as the location for two 'secret' gigs at Lampeter University and Theatr Gwynedd in Bangor, on 9 and 10 May respectively. Word inevitably got around the fan grapevine and, despite the supposedly secret nature of these shows, the small venues were packed, and despite some reported teething troubles the shows were apparently extremely good.

With these test shows out of the way, the band were confident to embark on their first run of serious live work since getting back together, with a tour of France, along with a couple of diversions to Switzerland and Belgium, taking up most of May. One problem at this juncture was that Hugh Banton was now having notable problems with his teeth, and by the time he saw a dentist about the toothache, he was told he would need a series of appointments to fix it, but with the French trip coming up the treatment had to be put on hold for a month. He was, therefore, in some discomfort throughout the French tour, and was prescribed some strong painkillers to manage things, though while countering the pain, these also had the side effect of compromising his appetite and generally making him feel more than a little out of sorts. By the time of the final show in Liege on 1 June, Gordian Troeller (in the compilation *The Box*) claimed that they had to carry him onstage to his keyboard, but Hugh refutes this now, insisting it never quite got that bad:

No, I'm sure I didn't have to be carried onstage, some memories must be getting mixed up there. I had toothache, certainly, and painkillers, but that was it. I know there have been claims that I was self-medicating with alcohol, and even that I was drinking a bottle of vodka a day, but that wasn't the case at all. Can you even drink that much? I know I couldn't. The thing was, at that time, we had started getting backstage riders, whereby you asked for whatever food and drink you wanted and it would be supplied. Peter liked tequila, so he asked for that, and I said, 'Vodka.' And lo and behold, a full bottle would arrive backstage at every show. I'd open it and just have a sip or whatever, and that would be about it. Occasionally I'd take the bottle back to the hotel in case I wanted a drink later, but that was it. Whoever drank all the vodka, it certainly wasn't me!

The shows, for the most part, went quite smoothly, with the band very much on form, but of course, it wouldn't be Van der Graaf without a couple of disasters derailing things, and this was no exception. At a show in Montpellier, a theft of equipment forced the gig to be cancelled at almost the last minute, with David Jackson the thief's victim. As well as his regular flight cases, he had a smaller bag, similar to a briefcase, which contained small but essential items, including the harness and slings which held the two saxophones in place as he played, and also some vital electronics and effects which were pivotal to his playing. The suspicion was that whoever the thief was, he had mistaken the briefcase-looking item for a similar one filled with money and simply taken it in an opportune manner. If so, he must have been disappointed to find a stash of bespoke saxophone equipment which was useless to him, but that was small consolation to David or the band, as they simply couldn't play. Different methods of securing the instruments in place were tried unsuccessfully, but even if they had proved feasible, the lack of the electronic gadgetry rendered it impossible to put on a show which could even attempt to create the VdGG sound, such was their individuality by this time. John Goodman hastily rushed back to London to get replacements, even having to remake several of the items in his workshop, as they were bespoke one-off affairs, and the tour was able to continue.

A rather different set of circumstances happened when the band were set to play the Villerupt Festival early in the tour. Villerupt was (and presumably still is) actually a very small town – basically a glorified village – tucked away in the middle of nowhere on the way to Luxembourg, and the festival was a one-day affair organised by the local Communist Party, featuring Van der Graaf headlining over Ducks Deluxe and the openers, Dr Feelgood. Sean Tyla, from Ducks Deluxe, and later to front his own band, The Tyla Gang, remembers that Van der Graaf had to go on after them being the headliners, which was fine until the mighty Ducks broke down in Belgium when their hired Triumph 2000 decided it was going to travel no further, and a mechanic had to be called. Unable to restart the stricken Triumph, he took them to the festival site in a Mercedes, which would appear to have at least partially saved the day. Dr Feelgood, he says, had been holding the fort manfully for a lot longer than they were supposed to play, but they headed for the stage to relieve them, and the Ducks went on albeit somewhat later than planned. Unfortunately, at this very moment, owing to the Communist-backed nature of the event, a local fascist group were busy phoning the local police to inform them that they had planted a rather large bomb. Again, according to Tyla's account, they had been playing for around 15 minutes when the stage was invaded from the rear by what they at first took to be locals in fancy dress. In fact, they were actually real firemen searching for a bomb which might at any moment blow the stage sky-high. Cue the end of a rather truncated set, as the entire festival audience, and bands, were evacuated, only for it to transpire, unsurprisingly, that the call had been a hoax and there was no bomb. Everyone duly trooped back in again so that things could resume, but by now, things were running critically late, and Van der Graaf ended up playing a truncated set of around 45 minutes, though this was still around three times as long as Ducks Deluxe had managed.

When the band headed over to Switzerland for a show in St Gallen on 26 May, Guy Evans was surprised, to say the least, when he saw a poster advertising the show. The reason for this surprise was the wording 'Van der Graaf Generator, featuring Peter Hammill (piano/guitar/vocal), Hugh Banton (keyboards/bass), David Jackson (saxophone/flute) and Chris Judge Smith (drums). The discovery that Judge Smith had made a triumphant if unexpected return to the band mid-tour after six years would indeed have been a startling one, but thankfully news of Guy's sacking was exaggerated, and the poster a rather amusing error. Guy made sure to get hold of one of the posters, and gave it to Judge after the tour finished!

When it came to the final French shows in Paris, the band were very unusually booked to play at the Salle Wagram, which had the distinction of having been featured prominently in the film *Last Tango in Paris*, and rarely hosted rock bands. The reason for this came from a remark Guy had made to Gordian when they were arranging the tour dates, when he said that he really didn't care for the Olympia, which was the planned, and more usual, venue. He simply made a comment that somewhere with a different vibe to it 'such as the ballroom from *Last Tango in Paris*' would be a great alternative. Taking this as a challenge, Gordian simply went away, without telling anyone, and booked this sumptuously appointed Napoleonic ballroom for the show.

The band returned to England on 2 June and, after a week in which Hugh finally got his teeth attended to, they headed to Rockfield Studios on the 9th to begin recording the comeback album, which would be titled *Godbluff*. These sessions went extremely smoothly, and the album was completed in three weeks, wrapping up on the 29th. In fact, even more was completed as, in addition to the four tracks which would eventually make up the album, two additional songs were recorded as well. These two ('Pilgrims' and 'La Rossa') would be used for the following album *Still Life,* the next year. The four used were 'The Undercover Man', 'Scorched Earth', 'Arrow' and 'The Sleepwalkers'. Guy Evans remembers making the final decision on the album's tracklisting, which was agreed by all four members:

Well, we all agreed on the running order and the track selection, but I do remember this thing about sitting at the table with pieces of paper with track names and timings on them, just shuffling them around and trying different combinations. When I looked at that list of those four tracks as it ended up, I was just sure that was the one. It wasn't everybody's favourite at first because it was a pretty uncompromising selection – I think that taking those six tracks, including 'Pilgrims' and 'La Rossa', you could have possibly made a slightly more conventional, listener-friendly album out of them. If you wanted to get as far 'out there' as you could, those four would be it, but everyone ultimately agreed on that.

The album would be released later in the year, but for now, with the recording complete, it was time for more live work. Following a BBC session, recorded on 3 July and broadcast a week later, in which the band played 'Scorched Earth' and 'The Sleepwalkers' from the forthcoming album, and a one-off gig in France on the 22nd, it was time for the first show in England. The band appeared at the Victoria Palace in London on 27 July. This being in the pre-internet days, which seem increasingly like another lifetime now, many fans were still completely unaware that the band had even re-formed when the show was announced, and the resulting scramble for tickets brought an echo of the scenes of Italian madness in 1972, with one newspaper report claiming that up to a thousand fans were locked out, trying in vain to gain entry. People had travelled from all over Europe (and even further afield), and many of those locked out of the show were reportedly Italian fans who had travelled – so at least being locked outside might have made them feel at home, one might say! The show itself was a triumph, with almost all reports overwhelmingly enthusiastic. The band played all of the new album, of course, along with 'La Rossa', 'Man-Erg', 'Lemmings' and even four from Hammill's solo albums in the shape of 'Black Room', 'A Louse Is Not A Home', 'Forsaken Gardens' and 'Faint-Heart And The Sermon'. The encore consisted of 'Urban' mixed with a snippet of 'Nadir's Big Chance' followed by 'Pilgrims', which seems a very odd choice for a crowd-pleasing encore, since not only had the songs not yet been released, but in fact they were not even to be included on the forthcoming record. Such was (and still is) the dedicated nature of the VdGG fan base, however, that they were able to do this with scarcely a murmur of discontent.

The band were keen to get back to Italy to play, following their previous triumphant reception there, and also with *The Long Hello* having been released over there only (at that time), maintaining their connection with the country. This time out, however, they would find things a little trickier as Italy had become something of a lawless place, if reports are to be believed, with widespread political unrest between the Communist Party and the far right – not to mention the fact that many youths had begun to regard rock concerts as displays of capitalist greed, and consequently believed that they had the right to enter for nothing, as the music should be free. The police, of course, had other ideas about this concept of a Unitarian utopia, and would take every opportunity to display this fact. Full-scale riots had recently broken out at a Lou Reed gig (not the least confrontational of artists, of course, but even so…), and the storm clouds seemed to be gathering even before the band got to their first gig, which was promptly cancelled anyway. This was a different Italy to the one only three years earlier, but in the end, most of the shows went off without major incident – notwithstanding power problems at a show near Rimini and the misfortune of Hugh Banton managing to injure his right hand in almost *Spinal Tap* fashion while go-karting. The band deemed this fairly low-key jaunt around smaller, lower-profile venues to be a reasonable success, and thus made plans to return later in the year to some larger venues, which would not go quite as smoothly, to say the least.

For now, however, it was time to consider the UK again. A full tour was planned for October, but before that, a repeat show at the Victoria Palace was arranged for 30 August, partly to accommodate the overspill of the thousand or so disappointed fans who were locked out of the previous show – presumably they weren't still there mind you. The show was by most accounts not quite as good as the first one, but even though some reviews were decidedly mixed, none took a hammer to the performance with quite the gusto of a decidedly un-rock-and-roll-sounding journalist named Antony Thorncroft in the unlikely pages of the *Financial Times*. Opening with a description of the music as 'irritatingly tedious' in its 'complete absence of melody or consistent rhythm', the possibly-suit-wearing Thorncroft turned his derision on the audience who, he concluded, may well have been 'too drugged to care'. By now warming to his task, he painted a bleak picture of these ticket-holding denizens of the nearest opium den as having 'passively accepted a single encore and drifted out like lost souls into the night', but did conclude with a positive spin: it was, he trumpeted, a happy eventuality that this music was in the hands of such a 'strange and youthful minority', as it ensured a musical barrier 'which keeps out the trivial and the commercial, but also most of the threads that make for a worthwhile musical experience'. Well, that's all right then. It may help the appreciation of the above by imagining it printed on a nice pink shade of paper, nestled next to a report about an exciting rise in the share price of soybeans and cattle feed.

Another UK show in the rock and roll hotbed of Bracknell Sports Centre was followed by a few European gigs in Holland, Belgium and Switzerland, with a classic 'only in the world of Van der Graaf' accident happening on the short flight to Amsterdam, when a thermos flask was taken on board, as Hugh Banton recalled in *The Book*, 'and somebody had failed to realise that at 10,000 feet things boil. Someone opened the thermos and it went off.' Hugh received burns to his right shoulder, was met by the Red Cross at the show and remembers playing the gig bandaged up. A happier incident was at a gig in Charleroi, Belgium, which was filmed for Belgian TV. The film of the show featured all of the *Godbluff* tracks (though not the rest of the set, frustratingly), and was later widely released on video and DVD, often with the earlier film of 'A Plague Of Lighthouse Keepers' also included.

October was to be an important month, with the UK tour finally taking place, with 20 shows (at 20 different venues, unlike the double-show Italian dates) between 5 October in Liverpool and, back to almost the same place, Manchester on 2 November. That first show in Liverpool was the cause of more technical gremlins as, shortly after beginning the opening song, a power surge took out the lights and the sound and rendered Hugh Banton's organ completely inoperative. After a bizarre interlude in which the other three fought to keep the crowd entertained with 45 minutes of improvisational jamming, the show was able to at last get back underway. Also, in October, *Godbluff* was finally released to an expectant fan base. And they received it enthusiastically.

The album, consisting of just two tracks on each side of vinyl originally, is a dynamically live-sounding piece of work. For this precise reason, Guy Evans names it as his favourite VdGG album, with the more organic feel of the record being closer in spirit to how they played live as a band. Opening (as the shows would do that year) with 'The Undercover Man', the album enters on a quietly contemplative note before the band kick in with some thrilling ensemble playing in a piece which develops brilliantly between its component parts. When it ends on a powerful note, that momentum is maintained into 'Scorched Earth', as one piece flows straight from the other. The latter song ups the intensity with some astoundingly intense vocal delivery from Peter Hammill. It's an astonishing side of music to re-enter the arena with, and things don't let up on the second half of the album. 'Arrow' opens with some almost free-form introductory sax and drum work which sounds improvised – and partially it is. In fact, Guy Evans' free-jazz drumming in this section came about entirely by accident. The sessions had become long and protracted, and he was getting frustrated with playing the planned drum part to the section, so out of frustration, he played a completely different part which he essentially made up on the spot. Everyone liked it, and so it stayed. Another powerful song, 'Arrow' leads into what many regard as the real main course of the album, the epic, over-ten-minute 'The Sleepwalkers', which features some of Hammill's finest lyrics to date, combining a meditation on the world of dreams and sleeping with the analogy of man as a species 'sleepwalking' through life even when awake. Are we ever truly awake, he seems to be asking, and if not, what is the nature of our existential dream state? Musically the song goes all over the map, with one startling section suddenly cutting disorientatingly into a quirky, tea-dance cha-cha-cha interlude which somehow, against all of the rules of conventional musicality, manages to work perfectly – or at least once the listener's initially shell-shocked brain can process it! Lyrically, a whole chapter could be taken up by an examination of Hammill's lyrics on this album. Dense, profound and yet deliberately obfuscated to just the right degree to encourage individual interpretation of the words, the progress here from the already excellent yet still occasionally clumsy couplets of five years previously is astonishing. This is the point at which the lines between Peter Hammill, the songwriter and Peter Hammill, the poet, begin to blur into almost invisibility.

The cover of the album was deliberately designed in a stark, functional way. The front and back covers (no gatefold here) are both black, with the rear bearing four photos of the individual members and the front a new band logo, clearly inspired by the optical-illusionary artwork of M.C. Escher. Also on the front is the title in red, diagonally beneath the band name as if rubber-stamped onto it in the manner of a visa in a passport. The inner sleeve contains the lyrics, but there is nothing remotely sumptuous here – entirely by design, as they wanted to keep it stripped back and basic. The title is an intriguing one, but there is a story behind it, as Guy explains:

It was a sort of a wry comment, I suppose you might say. We were known for being a little bit obscure, and perhaps a bit verbose, when we were being interviewed. It always used to be particularly notable in Germany for some reason; we always seemed to face these interviews, which tended to be deep and at length. There was always a question along the lines of 'how would you describe your music?', and where some people would say 'prog' or 'rock' or whatever, we couldn't really do that as we were pretty much self-defining! So to stump them a bit, when they asked the question, expecting at least about half an hour of earnest stuff coming out of us, we would just say 'Oh, it's godbluff!' as a bit of an in-joke. So the phrase was around at that time, and the whole sound of the record fed into the nature of the sleeve design as well. I can remember being very taken with the stripped-back idea of the sound being a reflection of how we played rather than the studio, and that sparse black-and-silver design seemed to fit that rather well. I think I came up with the idea of the rubber stamp effect of the title, sort of 'File Under Godbluff' if you like.

****

Following the album's release and the end of the UK tour, the band headed back over to Europe again. Following a few shows in France, they headed back to Italy, where, following the relatively successful nature of the earlier shows there, they planned a tour of slightly bigger and grander venues. This time, however, it was all going to end up in a scenario that even this most chaotic of bands could never have envisioned.

The first gig began reasonably, but before very long, the stage and the backstage area were invaded by the political protesters who had been feared at the earlier shows. The venue in question was a large glass and metal building with a prefabricated stage, and the band's truck was actually being used as the dressing room, kitted out with tables and refreshments etc., and backed up to the side of the stage area, so that the band could simply walk out of the back of the truck and on to the stage. Not long after they had started playing, they were alarmed, to say the least, at the sight of a large number of people wearing stocking masks and carrying batons, who headed for the stage and climbed into the lighting rig, hurling nuts and bolts, and even bricks, which were raining down onto the stage. Guy:

There was, in fact, a little more to it than that, as we later had it confirmed to us that these people were actually paid to riot and disrupt the show as a political gesture, as we were seen to be broadly aligned with the left wing and so it was organised to sabotage the gig. In fact, I think we left the stage once and then tried again – they invaded the backstage area first, but when that was repelled, we went back and tried to continue, but when the debris started flying, we had to run for our own safety to the truck.

Having got into the relative safety of the mobile dressing room, however, things were far from over. The driver of the truck – possibly because he just wanted to get the band out of there, or perhaps because he was being attacked himself, according to Guy – was in no mood to hang around. The doors, however, which were made of glass set into a glass wall, remained resolutely closed, and so in the manner of a scene you might more reasonably expect to find in a TV drama, he took matters into his own hands and floored the accelerator. The truck was, of course, stronger and heavier than the glass, and so it simply crashed through the wall and kept going, with the hapless musicians in the back, able to see the glass raining down through the translucent roof of the back area. The road crew, by this time, had armed themselves with coshes made from gaffer tape, but by all accounts, most of the violence ceased at the spectacle of a ten-ton truck driving straight through the wall, and the equipment was intact and able to be collected later.

In the meantime, the band were utterly disoriented by where they now were, and both Gordian and Guy maintain that when the truck came to a stop, they believed that they might well have simply driven round to the other side of the venue and still be in the thick of the trouble. For some reason which probably made sense at the time, they had all dressed in matching blue boiler suits for the show, and when they came to a stop, and heard voices outside, Gordian and Guy both remember picking up anything they could to defend themselves (Guy recalls having a cymbal stand), and when the back doors were opened they leapt out prepared for a fight. In actual fact, the driver had made his way to the car park of a nearby cinema, and when the middle-aged people quietly queueing for a film saw four boiler-suited men leap from the back of a truck, they apparently scattered in understandable alarm!

Hugh Banton remembers this slightly differently, though agrees on the main points:

We certainly crashed through the wall, but I am sure we must have known we were away from the venue by the time we stopped, and I certainly don't remember any weapons being grabbed exactly. Mind you, I do remember having fallen to the floor of the truck, seeing David's flute flying straight for me and grabbing it exactly in the manner of a

Star Wars lightsaber! It was a cinema, though, that's quite true, and I suppose looking back at it, four men in boiler suits emerging from the back of a truck covered in glass and debris must have seemed a little bit intimidating!

The last word on that particular incident must go to the promoter who, as Gordian has recounted it, was memorably unfazed by the whole experience. As he stated in *The Book*, 'I dropped the band off and went back… I was shaking like a leaf, I didn't know whether the building had collapsed or what I might find… Everyone was all right, but there was smashed glass everywhere. I asked the promoter what we should do… and he just said to me, 'I must get that door sign-posted better!''

One would have expected that to be enough excitement for one tour, but that was going to be far from the case. The next two shows, both in Genoa, went ahead without incident, but unsurprisingly the road crew, in particular, were in a far from relaxed mood, and there was an edgy atmosphere, to say the least. The following day there was a show at the Palasport stadium in Rome, a venue which had been the scene of a lot of trouble not too long before when Lou Reed had appeared, and everybody was very wary, especially when the 5,000 ticket-holders expected turned into 16,000, and there was a heavy police presence, but all went off without notable incident. The band went for a meal after the show and returned to the hotel, with the truck parked nearby for the road crew to leave in early the next morning for the long drive to the next show, up in Bologna. Come the morning, the roadies headed out to where the truck had been parked, only to find that there was no truck, simply a space where it had been left with all of the band's gear locked inside.

The driver informed Gordian what had happened, who then passed the word on to the band, and everyone was momentarily taken aback as to what they should do. Not for long, however, as very soon, a phone call came in. The truck had been taken and was being held to ransom, with a demand for a figure variously remembered as £10,000 or £20,000 for its return. No matter what the figure, they didn t have it, and the matter was immediately put in the hands of the police. After a while, however, it was taken back out of their hands, as they didn't appear to be doing anything to actually progress the investigation. Frustrated, Gordian took matters upon himself and began organising search parties, with him and the road crew going out in cars to scour the city, communicating with each other via walkie-talkies.

After failing to locate the missing vehicle, an idea struck Gordian. He suddenly remembered – as you do, or in most cases, absolutely don't – that he had an ex-girlfriend in London who happened to know a rather high-ranking mafia figure in the USA, so he promptly phoned her up and asked her if she could call her friend and just enquire as to whether he knew anything about it, and whether it had any mob connection. That's friends in high places for you, I suppose! Anyway, sure enough, he got a call back in the middle of the night from a man with a strong New York accent who informed him that it was nothing to do with them, but that it was, in fact, 'amateurs'. He went on to suggest that they should look north of Rome, and more or less provided the location of where the truck might be.

Armed with this information, he went to the police and they offered to lead him to where the truck was said to be. He followed them onto the motorway, whereupon they immediately roared away at high speed and tried to lose him! He managed to keep up with them by dint of some desperate and probably rather hazardous driving, and followed them to a pound-cum-scrap yard where the truck was indeed locked up. He maintains that the police were in on the whole thing, as he claims that while he spoke Italian, they did not realise that, and he overheard the police saying to the man in charge of the pound that 'you really screwed up this time', which does sound rather incriminatory in all fairness. Once again, Guy Evans has his own memory of this:

That all ties in, you see, to the slightly uneasy relationship that existed, certainly at the time, between the Carabinieri, who are the sort of paramilitary police, and the Vigili, who are the regular police as we know them. What we were given to understand is that there were effectively 'bent' Carabinieri who would arrange for vehicles to be stolen, which would then be taken to this sort of breaker's yard where they would be stripped of all saleable assets and contents, whereupon the owners would then be informed that what was left of it had 'miraculously' been found. When our truck was found, unfortunately, Peter's guitar and my drum kit had disappeared, never to return.

Sure enough, the police claimed that the VdGG truck had actually been found earlier, but owing to a failure in communication, nobody had been informed, and that they were as surprised as the band were that it was at that particular location. It isn't known for sure, but let us just say that suspicions remained extremely high. The roadies returned the following day with another battery (that had been stripped out, of course), and one of them happened to look under a nearby pile of tyres, only to find a missing transformer there. Before he could retrieve it, he was spotted by the workers at the pound, and they were chased away from their own truck by a mob armed with iron bars.

At this point, there was something of a delay as the VdGG contingent were unable to get to the truck, so they had no alternative but to rely on the police again, who, by now, of course had no choice to help whether they wanted to or not. They tried to get back there themselves, only to find the place guarded by a group of leather-jacketed 'heavies' preventing anyone going in. What was happening, it would seem, is that the mysteriously tyre-hidden transformer was being returned to the vehicle, as by the time the police arrived to arrange for the truck to be returned, it had mysteriously been replaced together with some other 'liberated' accessories, and all concerned were coming across as bewildered innocents in the whole affair. Peter's beloved ice-blue Stratocaster and Guy's treasured walnut Gretsch drum kit were never seen again, however, though there was one almost unbelievable stroke of luck. David Jackson had an enormous flight case which was nicknamed the 'Van Gogh', containing all of his saxophones, his electrical devices, and even his trademark hats, and the contents were an absolute dream for opportunist thieves. However, owing to the size and appearance of it, it had been mistaken for one of the PA cabinets (which were too unwieldy to be worth stealing), and had therefore been left there untouched the whole time. It may have been a silver lining only, but it was certainly something.

By this time, the events had been reported at home in England. In fact, they had even been reported on the Radio 1 news bulletin, which Hugh Banton's wife Sue had been listening to. Unfortunately, the report got its wires crossed somewhat and dramatically announced that the members of Van der Graaf Generator had been kidnapped in Italy and were being held to ransom! Having been married for only around six months, this naturally alarmed Sue Banton to the extent that frantic transcontinental telephone calls were required for Hugh to reassure her that, no, they had not been kidnapped and were quite safe, even if the truck was not.

Of course, the rest of the tour was cancelled. Absurdly, attempts were made to persuade the band to fulfil the remaining shows using hired equipment, but this was never going to happen. For one thing, their equipment was entirely geared to their own specifications, but even apart from that, the trauma from those three shows must have been immense. When they left, they were given a police escort out of Rome, with it being left in no doubt that they should get out of the city immediately, and they were accompanied to leave nothing open to chance. On the drive back, the truck driver was reportedly so stressed and strung out that he refused to drive at all unless they were in a convoy, with the roadies in front of him in one car and the band with Gordian in another behind him. They eventually arrived home on 8 December, a week after the theft.

That would be enough for anyone to deal with, one would imagine, but then again, this is a story about Van der Graaf Generator, and there is always one more cosmic punch for the universe to deliver. Peter Hammill, already reeling from the loss of his guitar and the whole week-long nightmare, returned home to discover that his long-time partner Alice had left him in the meantime and gone off with someone who was a former roadie for the band. This final blow stunned him so much that he was in a rather dark place for some time, and he would go on to channel the experience into his next solo album, *Over*, which would function as a cathartic exorcism of the end of the relationship. In fact, in the wake of all of this, the band members were keeping their distance from each other as any interaction was understandably raking up the whole thing in their minds. Unbelievably, however, they did play one more show before the end of the year, in Hemel Hempstead on 18 December, and while they remembered it less than fondly (in particular David Jackson who recalled it as being 'appalling'), the appearance of a recording of the show revealed it, even to the band themselves, to have actually been astonishingly powerful, with all manner of demons being forcibly driven out through the intensity of the music. It may have been a great show, but at what cost!

With the year coming to a close, the reunion, which had seemed set fair for avoidance of all of the old pitfalls from the earlier incarnation of the band, had ended up immeasurably more traumatic than anything that had gone before. The music had continued to be exceptional, perhaps better than ever, but would that be enough as the band limped into 1976, licking their collective wounds?

1976 – Now The Immortals Are Here

Still Life
Personnel:
Peter Hammill: vocals, piano, guitar
David Jackson: saxophone, flute
Hugh Banton: organ, bass, mellotron, piano
Guy Evans: drums and percussion
Recorded at Rockfield Studios, June 1975 and January 1976
Produced by Van der Graaf Generator
Released: 15 April 1976 (UK: Charisma, US: Mercury)
Highest chart places: Did not chart
Running time: 44:57
Tracklisting:
1. 'Pilgrims' (Hammill, Jackson) 7.12, 2. 'Still Life' (Hammill) 7.25, 3. 'La Rossa' (Hammill) 9.53, 4. 'My Room (Waiting For Wonderland)' (Hammill) 8.03, 5. 'Childlike Faith In Childhood's End' (Hammill) 12.24

World Record
Personnel:
Peter Hammill: vocals, piano, guitar
David Jackson: saxophone, flute
Hugh Banton: organ, bass pedals, mellotron
Guy Evans: drums and percussion
Recorded at Rockfield Studios, May 1976
Produced by Van der Graaf Generator
Released: October 1976 (UK: Charisma, US: Mercury)
Highest chart places: Did not chart
Running time: 52:19
Tracklisting:
1. 'When She Comes' (Hammill) 8.02, 2. 'A Place To Survive' (Hammill) 10.05, 3. 'Masks' (Hammill) 7.10, 4. 'Meurglys III, The Songwriter's Guild' (Hammill) 20.51, 5. 'Wondering' (Banton, Hammill) 6.36

As 1975 rolled into 1976, things were not in the best of shape in terms of band morale – Peter Hammill, in particular, had suffered a double blow, while the four group members all took a little time to themselves and let the dust settle, so to speak. It didn't settle for long, however, as that break for things to heal somewhat lasted until the first week in January, whereupon it was back onto the horse and into rehearsals for the next album. This seems a shockingly brief period to have as a necessary break, but there were plans and deadlines aplenty. Asked whether the events of the past couple of months had seriously threatened to derail the band's reunion (especially since it had taken Peter so long to come around to the idea), Guy Evans is quite certain that wouldn't have been on the cards:

I don't think so, no. The thing was, there was so much creative momentum carrying us forward at the time that I don't think we even considered for a moment getting off. Plus, of course, there were financial pressures driving us on, especially after the Italian tour getting abandoned. We were too much in hock still, I think! No, it would have been very disappointing at that point to have packed it up.

Rehearsals took place at Clearwell Castle and were shorter than would generally be the case for a new album because, of course, two songs ('Pilgrims' and 'La Rossa') were already recorded and complete, having been left off *Godbluff*. That meant around 17 minutes of the music for the album was complete and had no more work needing to be done, and there were just three new songs to work out and record. After the rehearsals, the band went straight into Rockfield Studios to record the new material, which was all finished, remarkably, before the end of January. Hugh Banton, in particular, remembers this as being a good time – his wife Sue had come to the studio and brought their cats with her, and the events of the previous December were receding a little. Guy Evans, however, was less content; having to record using rented drums was not making the process any easier for him, and he found himself yearning for the more 'live' and less clinically studio-bound atmosphere of *Godbluff*. His does seem to have been the lone discontented tone, as one might put it, as Banton and Jackson both claim to have been very happy with proceedings.

The recording sessions wrapped up on 25 January, following which, in February, the band set out on a tour of France to showcase much of the new material (though some had already been played live the previous year, of course). Support for the tour was, in a somewhat bizarre pairing, veteran blues musician Alexis Korner. Already approaching 50 years old, Korner had been around the British blues scene for decades, notably fronting his band Blues Incorporated – although he was most familiar to 1970s teenagers without most of them even knowing it. His experimental 'big band' CCS (which stood for Collective Consciousness Society) were responsible for the horn-driven version of Led Zeppelin's 'Whole Lotta Love' which was used as the theme tune to the TV show *Top of the Pops* for most of the decade, but despite that departure into an oddly listener-friendly jazz-rock sound, he always remained a bluesman in the same manner as John Mayall and was sometimes given the title 'the Godfather of British blues'. Needless to say, while his appearance was a delight for the band (and acolyte David Jackson in particular), the audience were less enthralled (they 'weren't hip to him', as Hugh Banton later noted. 'Perhaps they should have been, but they weren't'), and despite Korner showing VdGG the utmost respect, and watching their performances, he left the tour after a few dates, stating that it wasn't really 'his scene', which is probably a fair comment.

March brought only one live appearance, this time a Peter Hammill solo show at the New Theatre, Oxford, on the 26th. It was notable for the premiering of some new songs which would be recorded for his next solo album *Over*. Along with these cathartic songs of despair inspired by the departure of Alice, the show also marked the first performance of a song which would appear later in the year on the next Van der Graaf album *World Record*, called 'Meurglys III'. It was a far cry from the lengthy band version of the piece, being as it was simply Hammill on acoustic guitar and vocal, but by all accounts, it was a high point of the show. Another series of UK shows by the band took place in April and early May, but before that the band had recorded yet another John Peel session, performing 'Still Life' and 'La Rossa' in breathtaking style. Guy Evans, in particular, had a good reason for enjoying the session, as it coincided with a replacement drum kit courtesy of the Charisma purse strings, which brought him considerable joy. As he explains now:

Ever since the old kit was stolen from the van, I'd had to use hired kits, including for the recording of the *Still Life* album. Nowadays, if you hire a kit, as long as you specify it well enough, you're pretty much guaranteed to get something pretty good. Back then, it was very different, and you could end up with any sort of beaten-up old thing. I went along to Pro Perc, which was the big hire company at the time, looking to see if there was anything I could bear to use. It was so bad that at times you would actually get completely dysfunctional items which simply didn't work. Anyway, this Gretsch kit came in, which was really close to my old one. It wasn't new, as it had been used by Lenny White from Return To Forever, but it was a lovely kit, so I asked about hiring it, but they said it was for sale only. So I settled for whatever else was the least worst option for this Peel session, and I thought that was it, but when it arrived and I opened up the flight cases, it was this Gretsch kit in there, which was rather great!

Shortly after that session, on 15 April, *Still Life* was released. Even today, it stands up as a remarkable piece of work, even among the standard of the Van der Graaf Generator catalogue of the time, with its five tracks each representing perfectly a different facet of what made the band such a unique proposition. 'Pilgrims' is an inspired choice as opener, having an uplifting, effortlessly propulsive quality to it, which is utterly irresistible. Peter Hammill's voice is in magisterial form here, and also listen towards the end of the track for a drum fill from Guy Evans, which is absolutely sublime. Following that comes the brilliant wordsmithery of the title track, speculating on a future in which science has conquered death, only for the promised paradise of eternity to become an eternal, hellish prison of ennui and stultifying, inescapable inertia. You weren't getting that sort of thing from any old rock album, even in the endlessly fertile musical landscape of the 1970s! The other track recorded along with 'Pilgrims' at the *Godbluff* sessions, 'La Rossa', closes the first side of vinyl in what is a coruscating outpouring of frustration followed by a mixture of relief and despair, as Hammill dissects a treasured platonic relationship which he knows is about to be destroyed forever if the people concerned turn it into a physical coupling. Spoiler alert: they do, and it doesn't end well.

The second side opens with the languorously beautiful 'My Room (Waiting For Wonderland)', which sees a reflective Hammill ruminating on the hope he yearns for in his despairing mental and emotional position. It's simultaneously upliftingly hopeful and cathartically hopeless at the same time, without ever rising above a restrained and yet aching beauty. This line-up never performed the song live, though Hammill has done so frequently in solo shows, at the piano. Closing the album is the longest track, the 12 and a half minutes of epic drama which is 'Childlike Faith In Childhood's End'. Both David Jackson and Hugh Banton have named this as being right at the top of their favourite VdGG pieces, and for good reason, as the meditation on the future and evolution of mankind is both labyrinthine in its structure and also incredibly stirring at its most elegiac moments. Everything you could want from Van der Graaf Generator is encapsulated on this album, and yet Charisma bizarrely marketed it in a decidedly low-key and half-hearted fashion. Hugh Banton said: 'Charisma just didn't get behind the album for some reason. *Godbluff* had quite a bit of publicity, but when *Still Life* came out, they basically said, "This is a stopgap album for Van der Graaf Generator." Well, it wasn't! It was an album we had put a lot into, and I would probably say that it is still my favourite of our albums. We never did stopgap albums, and we certainly didn't that time.'

The album came once again in a non-gatefold single sleeve, though the cover was somewhat more eye-catching than the rather sparse *Godbluff* design, with the front cover image initially causing much discussion about what exactly it was. Some fans speculated that it might be a fern of some kind or a highly stylised photo of a network of rivers, but in fact, the answer was a much more appropriate one for the band: discovered by David Jackson in a magazine, the photo is in fact a spark from an actual Van de Graaff generator machine, captured in acrylic and frozen. Thus, it rather neatly encapsulated both the band name and the 'Still Life' concept itself. The rear cover featured the lyrics in silver-on-black print, with the four band members' heads in double-exposure photographs below.

Despite Charisma's unfathomable dismissal of the album, it actually sold a respectable amount, racking up some 15,000 sales in the first couple of weeks – which may not exactly be in the *Tubular Bells* or *Dark Side Of The Moon* ballpark, but for the area in which an uncompromising band such as VdGG were operating, it was pretty good, all things considered. The band immediately headed out on a series of UK shows in April and May to promote the record, a jaunt which began with two dates at London's Roundhouse on 18 and 19 April. Support for those two nights was, interestingly enough, The 101ers and The Spiders From Mars. The latter band were something of a misleading proposition, being a new band put together by David Bowie's original Spiders From Mars rhythm section of future Uriah Heep bassist Trevor Bolder and drummer Woody Woodmansey. Misleading because, in those pre-internet days of music papers and word of mouth, many people would have seen only the name and gone along excitedly expecting to see Bowie and guitarist Mick Ronson, which could only put the band on the back foot immediately, one would imagine. The 101ers are best known now as the band which featured Joe Strummer before he went on to form The Clash later that year, and who had a well-regarded single release called 'Keys To Your Heart'. They didn't impress the Van der Graaf faithful by all accounts, leading Strummer to later ruefully reflect that despite them putting everything into a tight, fast and high-energy set, they simply couldn't impress the crowd, before commenting memorably that 'Mind you, I don't know what sort of music Van der Graaf is. It's like Shakespeare crossed with Uriah Heep.' Which may not be accurate, but you know what he meant!

Following those dates came four shows in early May, taking in Birmingham, Sheffield, Manchester and, finally, Bangor, Wales. These were all very successful gigs themselves, but this being Van der Graaf World, there was still room for an incident, as a stop-off at a motorway service station on the way back from one of the shows saw Gordian Troeller get into an argument with an intoxicated and belligerent individual, who promptly went on to attack him with a plastic cutlery knife in a frenzied yet bizarre manner, which left Gordian bleeding from a wound above the eye and the drunken miscreant apprehended by security and the police called. Cue the weary band members heading off to the police station to give witness statements until the early hours.

In the aftermath of these shows, and the plastic blade-wielding maniac, the band astonishingly devoted the remainder of the month to rehearsing, recording and mixing yet another new album, all within three weeks. The album, the final one released by the classic four-piece line-up until decades later, would be titled *World Record*, but would not see its release until October. The amount of material which was being produced by the band, and Peter Hammill in particular, at this time, was remarkable, with Van der Graaf now having recorded three studio albums of extraordinary quality in the space of around 12 months. Guy Evans has an interesting angle on this:

> The thing is, you say about the three albums in such a short time, but as well as the creative inspiration which we certainly had, there was also a sort of motivation to get things done while we could, because Van der Graaf was always unpredictable and liable to fall apart at any moment. While we were together and firing on all cylinders, we felt a real drive to capitalise on it while we could.

The first half of June then saw another trip over to the continent, with some Swiss gigs being followed by two festival dates in Germany. The festival in question was The Sunrise Festival, which unusually took place twice, in Offenburg on the 6th, and then again in Hamburg two days later, albeit in a truncated form. The Offenburg show was an all-day outdoor event with a remarkable bill, which saw Wishbone Ash headlining along with Bob Marley and the Wailers, The Kinks, Stephen Stills, War, Man and, of course, VdGG. The Hamburg show was a three-band affair only, with Wishbone Ash, War and VdGG third on the bill, held in the evening in the Ernst Merck Halle venue. On the 7th, the day in between these two German shows, the band clearly decided that a day off would simply be an excuse for idle sloth, and consequently headed over to the unlikely destination of Liechtenstein, for a show in the capital, Vaduz (which, as anyone who has visited that tiny principality will be aware, is to all intents and purposes the only city). In fact they received a large cake from the Arch Duke, which is certainly something else to put in the 'Only Van der Graaf...' column.

At this time, the band actually began chartering their own plane. With several dates like these festivals and the prospect of endless overnight car journeys, they found the cheapest charter company they could, which offered what Guy recalls as being 'very old aircraft'. Gordian sorted all of the arrangements out, and compared to the gruelling motorway journeys they had been used to, even an old aircraft was a huge improvement. Not that it was entirely straightforward, as Hugh Banton recalled the lack of what would be termed health and safety regulations today: 'The pilot used to let us have a go. So you'd be flying along and suddenly have this horrible realisation that you're being flown at 10,000 feet by Peter Hammill, who had just had a smoke...'

****

Later in June, David and Sue Jackson welcomed their first child, Jake, into the world, which prompted even this band to take a break of a month, though not before the Jacksons were presented with a 'Van der Graaf Generator pram', which was apparently envisioned as being recycled later for further Van der Graaf-generated offspring, though this pram-sharing dynasty did not quite come to pass. This was a welcome break for David Jackson in particular – and, to be blunt, a necessary one, as he has spoken of how difficult it had become juggling family and band life while things were so busy. Peter Hammill, of course, had other ideas while this month's rest was going on; he recorded another solo album. This would not be released until the following year, with the title *Over*, and contained all of the cathartic break-up songs concerning the Alice situation (which, let us not forget, was still only six months previous to this, though it seems almost as if half a lifetime had elapsed). This meant that Hammill had composed, rehearsed and recorded four albums' worth of material since the previous June, just about exactly 12 months. On this occasion, Peter went to the Foel Studio, where *The Long Hello* had been recorded, along with fellow contributors Dave Anderson and Ian Gomm. Most of the instrumental work was done by Hammill himself, but he was abetted on some tracks by Nic Potter and Guy Evans, along with violin from Graham Smith, who will very shortly enter this story in a significant way.

With the recording taking place with a small, select group of trusted friends and colleagues at a small, out-of-the-way yet familiar studio such as Foel, at least one would imagine that the recording would be free from any major incident. This belief would be to forget the Lords Of Chaos which followed the Van der Graaf Generator team around, however. Shortly after recording commenced, during the longest spell of sunny, dry weather in living memory, the studio was struck by lightning…

When the strike occurred, Ian Gomm was at the desk while Peter was recording the highly emotional song 'Alice (Letting Go)'. He had just finished, and was, Ian recalls, emotionally drained by it, when by the first astonishing coincidence, the phone rang, and when Ian answered, it was actually Alice asking to speak to Peter. He left Peter in the control room upstairs on the phone and went downstairs himself, and it was at that moment that he heard a clap of thunder, and saw the farmhouse next to the studio building struck by a huge lightning bolt. Followed by another hitting the studio.

Dave Anderson, relating the story in *The Book*, recalls how he was actually in the downstairs toilet having a pee when the strike happened. He looked down and saw, to his horror, sparks a foot long coming off the floor, swearing that they looked exactly like the shape of a letter Z, like giant cartoon sparks. He managed, he explained, to stop what he was doing very quickly (no doubt afraid of the sparks travelling up the flow!), and ran to the window to look outside. What he saw then was astonishing: 'I looked out and saw this huge great ball of fire hit right in the middle of the lawn, and then all these other smaller balls fly off all over the place, and I saw one of them hit the porch of my cottage and it burst into flames. Then I could see my wife running out with my six-year-old child. It was unbelievable, like Armageddon! There was only one cloud in the sky for six months, and it happened to be right over the studio during that track.'

Meanwhile, things were getting even more alarming in the studio itself, as Ian Gomm recalled: 'The lights went out and a luminous blue streak of lightning came in through the open studio door and shot up the inside wall towards the electricity fuse box. Peter had come running downstairs saying the phone had gone dead.' Dave Anderson further recalls the studio desks all getting burnt out, and the three of them sitting on the wooden stairs because it was the only place they felt safe, after the sparks leaping from the ground. When it was over, they all took an enormous shot from a bottle of vodka they had, and decided not to have another go at recording that song...

At the end of July, Van der Graaf were back in harness again, with a run of three shows at the Marquee being followed by a trip over to France for a festival in an old amphitheatre venue, and on 28 August, an appearance at the Reading Festival. The weather gods intervened again for that one as the band took to the stage after an enormous downpour. Shortly after starting the first song, they had to stop because Peter Hammill was inaudible, and it turned out that water had got into the sound system, and it had to be fixed – compere John Peel having the unenviable task of explaining that to an impatient crowd. When the band returned, they played a truncated set, but surprised their fans by ending with 'Killer', which they had not played for around five years, to make up for the problems. The result was a very well-received show indeed.

September saw a couple more UK shows in London and Edinburgh, before they headed off to the continent again for a tour of Holland and Belgium – a trip notable for the fact that Hugh Banton attempted to use the still unfinished HB1 organ on a tour like that for the first time; something which was fraught with technical difficulties. HB1 actually contained a whole section of the old Hammond E112 within it and was, as Hugh described it, a little like having about four organs in one, and, therefore, incredibly difficult to keep in tune, though it was improved by constant tweaking. It had a tendency to overheat so, a little like a computer with a malfunctioning cooling fan, they had to take the side off the organ so that it could get enough ventilation.

In fact, roadie Pete Donovan remembers that at most shows, John Goodman would be lying on the floor underneath the instrument with his legs sticking out like a car mechanic, tweaking something within the workings. Somehow, however, it worked. As Hugh remembers that time now:

At last, the all-too-brief debut of HB1. The organ contained the original Hammond keyboards and generators from the E112 of 1970–72, coupled with three newly designed electronic generator sets intended to provide all the Farfisa sounds and more, intended to be the ultimate rock/church organ. The American RTR cabinets utilised 24" bass speakers, at the time the only way to reproduce true 32-foot (16Hz) organ tone; much hyped in the music press at the time.

After that trip, in October, *World Record* was finally released. The longest of the three post-reunion albums, it came in at over 52 minutes, which was long for the vinyl format. It perfectly illustrated just how much quality material the band were able to put out at this time, as those three albums released within 12 months contained almost 140 minutes of new music, all of which was of the highest quality. The album opener is the strident 'When She Comes', reinforcing Guy Evans' view that the record was another very 'live'-sounding one. The lyric revolves around the mysterious lady 'with her skin so white', who is variously described as 'like something out of Edgar Allan Poe' and, less obviously, 'like something out of Blake or Burne-Jones'. For anyone who may be unsure of the latter, Edward Burne-Jones (1833–98) was an artist who was part of the Pre-Raphaelite Brotherhood, celebrated for his paintings and also, in particular, his work in stained glass (I can remember getting quite excited when visiting a Welsh church and seeing a window credited to Burne-Jones!). Following this, 'Place To Survive' may be the hardest-rocking track on this pretty abrasive album, with its lyrical message practically a self-help book delivered by four musical madmen, the exhortations to 'stand straight' and 'be strong' accompanied by driving, aggressive music which sounds as if it might be what would be popular heavy rock in an alternative world in which the 1960s had been dominated by Frank Zappa and Captain Beefheart rather than The Beatles and The Stones. After about six of its ten minutes, the regular 'song' portion departs to resolve into a thrillingly exuberant coda. Closing the original first side is 'Masks', an intense and uncompromising track written back in 1974 at the time of the *Godbluff* material but held over until now. Delving into the identity and sense of self by means of an extended metaphor regarding the wearing of various 'masks', it is one of the tracks which most exemplifies the increased amount of electric guitar played by Peter Hammill. It is clear by now that the preponderance of that instrument is one of the elements which most gives the album its relatively raw, live-sounding and, indeed, almost hard-rocking feel.

The second side opens with what could easily have filled an entire vinyl side of a typical-length album, the almost 21-minute 'Meurglys III, The Songwriter's Guild'. The rather oblique title refers to the 'Meurglys' name, which Hammill had given to various electric guitars since the very first Meurglys back in 1969. Hammill's current guitar at the time, Meurglys III itself, was unsurprisingly a black guild model. For the first two-thirds of its length, the piece is a fascinatingly complex exploration of the psyche of the protagonist who, being clearly in a fragile mental state ('these days I mainly talk to plants and dogs'), retreats more and more to coexist only with his guitar as company, before appearing to give himself a sort of virtual finger-wagging 'pep talk' which may, or may not do anything to rouse him from his torpor. It's a marvellous piece both musically and lyrically, but for the final eight minutes or so takes a bizarre left turn even for Van der Graaf, lurching into a lengthy reggae coda with Hammill firing off a guitar solo which, while it would not exactly cause sleepless nights for Carlos Santana or David Gilmour, is in fairness not intended to. Many fans felt, however, and still do, that the section does outstay its welcome a little by being over-extended. Guy Evans agreed with this when I asked him about it, but offered an interesting explanation for it:

Yes, I suppose it possibly does go on a little too long, but it was all down to our terrible, incurable penchant for in-jokes. You see, what's supposed to be happening there is that we were gradually falling apart, and it was pretty carefully orchestrated so that we'd start off playing in a fairly coherent fashion, and become gradually more fragmented as the thing went on. An example of an in-joke which probably wouldn't be clear to many people hearing it, I suppose!

Following that, and closing the album (and indeed the four-piece's final output for some decades) is the sublime 'Wondering', a track which is co-written between Hammill and Banton, seamlessly marrying Peter's wistfully nostalgic words looking back over time which has passed with Hugh's beautifully sympathetic and complementary music. There could not possibly have been a better sign-off, either for artist or band in general, and it remains one of their greatest achievements. There was even a video made for the track at the time, but it is not easily found, and, unsurprisingly, was not widely shown at the time.

The cover this time is far more straightforward than *Still Life*'s acrylic spark image had been, and certainly, nobody would have needed to guess about the glaringly obvious visual pun of a circular design which is made up half of the earth ('world') and half of a vinyl album ('record'). It looks quite nice, and is well done, but it doesn't fire the imagination. The back cover has the credits and, again, the lyrics in silver on black – the second time, the words have been on the back cover rather than on a printed inner sleeve. By 1976, of course, record company cutbacks were resulting in fewer and fewer gatefold cover extravaganzas, and unless you were seated at the very top table with the rarefied likes of Pink Floyd and Led Zeppelin, you had a pretty good chance of being limited to a non-gatefold single sleeve design. Each song was accompanied by a small thumbnail illustrating it; a woman's face from a painting for 'When She Comes', a sort of 'Vitruvian Man' posed figure against a vaguely mystical circle for 'A Place To Survive', a pair of Greek theatrical masks for 'Masks' (of course), a close up of Hammill's guitar for 'Meurglys III' and a stylised question mark for 'Wondering'.

As always there are some oddities in the credits, this time more so than there had been for some time. Hugh Banton is credited as 'Manuel and his Music of the Pedallos', while Peter Hammill is bafflingly listed as responsible for 'Vox, Meurglys III and Wassistderpunktenbacker. There are credits for 'aura', including nods to 'psychotic reaction, The Thing from behind the Wall, echoed lawnmower and The Ice Cream Man', and Gordian Troeller is, rather splendidly credited with 'Gordianisation'. Finally, and bereft of any obvious meaning whatsoever, we learn that 'The CONTROLLER was played by Splat Meringue, the MENTOR by Geept, and TREVOR by the Repertory Company'. Just in case you were wondering…

Following the baffling lack of promotion for *Still Life*, the seemingly schizoid Charisma this time swung into action again with a high-profile campaign advertising the album. Advertisements were placed in the music press showing a large 'V', in a – probably deliberate – very 'new wave' fashion (it looks rather reminiscent of the logo design used by the band The Vibrators as it happens). The V logo was accompanied by the rather odd message 'Van der Graaf Generator Is For Everyone', which really was about as far from reality as you could get. Whatever splendid qualities Van der Graaf possessed, appealing to the popular masses was not among them, and it is very difficult to imagine a world in which, like say *Jeff Wayne's War Of The Worlds* or *Abba's Greatest Hits*, people would remark that 'it seems every house you go into there's a copy of *World Record* by Van der Graaf Generator there.' It would have been nice, but snowballs would have had better holiday plans in hell. The Charisma PR machine even followed up this advertising campaign by producing badges with the V logo and the 'For Everyone' slogan on them. We shall assume that, this time out, they didn't consider it a 'stopgap release'...

As the album came out, another development on the gigging front was presenting itself, in the shape of a seven-date tour of Canada, followed by a single, high-profile showcase gig in New York, at the Beacon Theater on Broadway. With the band having never played in North America before at all (though Peter Hammill had, of course), this was somewhat unknown territory, though the indications were that they would probably do all right in Canada. In actuality, that was something of an understatement, as fans who had been waiting years for the chance to see the band resulted in scenes which at times were not a million miles from those Italian 'GeneratorMania' scenes of four years earlier. This was particularly true of the show in Quebec City, which drew a crowd estimated at over 6,000, and saw a return to the old days of rioting outside the venue. According to a local newspaper report, there were hundreds of fans waiting impatiently for the doors to open – which would have been fine, but for the fact that it was at that point 2 pm, with the actual show over five hours away!

Before this point in the tour, David Jackson had been trying to make contact with his wife's parents, as they were in Canada at the time. Her father, Ernest, was a very well-known dairy scientist, and they were in the country to attend a conference; David had been trying the phone number he had for them without success and was disappointed to have been unable to contact them. At the Quebec City show, however, he went on for the soundcheck in the afternoon, only to be amazed by the sight of his mother-in-law in the front row watching. He went to ask her what on earth was happening, only to find out that, by pure coincidence, the dairy conference was not only in Quebec, but actually in the same building on the same day! Apparently, Ernest was upstairs with the other delegates and colleagues, on the top floor, and they could see rioting youths below. Some of the people there were wondering whether there was trouble or some kind of demonstration going on, to which Ernest announced happily, 'Oh no. That's my son-in-law's band, Van der Graaf Generator! They're playing here.' They ended up attending the show and coming backstage where, according to David, they were 'very polite about declining joints and so on!'

There was an incident after one of the shows on the tour (believed to be in Rimouski, also in Quebec province) which was another of those 'only Van der Graaf' moments. At the hotel, the band and crew decided to draw lots for roommate pairing, and Pete Donovan ended up sharing with Guy Evans. He remembers waking up with a slightly confused vision of Guy outside the window, clinging to the windowsill. Thinking there must be an explanation for this, and not unaccustomed to such incidents, he rolled over and went back to sleep. He commented later that 'I found out over breakfast the next morning that Guy was trying to climb back in having somehow fallen out of the third-floor window, and was hoping for some assistance from me.'

Three days after the final Canadian date, in Toronto, with all of the band members having survived without any mortal injuries, the New York gig was scheduled to take place. It had been a bone of contention between Mercury, who had insisted on ploughing all of the money into making that one date a real showcase event, and the band, who were a little frustrated about being in the USA and doing only the one show. The frustration was only amplified when Frank Zappa got in touch with Gordian while the band were in Canada to ask about them doing a gig with him and the Mothers of Invention when they played in Buffalo, New York State. There had also been a gig over on the West Coast, which had been tentatively booked by a record company representative over there. But Mercury were adamant: they could not afford to finance any more shows as everything had been pumped into this one. In actual fact, that was certainly correct, as the band were treated like rock royalty, staying in the prestigious Essex House Hotel, Central Park West – so prestigious in fact that President Jimmy Carter was reportedly staying there at the same time. A huge reception was thrown after the sold-out and wildly successful show, with the great and the good of the press and celebrities turning out (not all with the same enthusiasm, perhaps, as Hugh Banton recalled 'I remember John Bonham arriving, going "Oh, right," and then leaving!') In fact, the band might have never even made it to the show had an incident on the way gone differently. David Jackson and Gordian Troeller were in a car with a driver on the way to the theatre, and when they stopped at a light, an old woman approached the car and asked for 95 cents change. Gordian and David were both counting out change as the former opened the window, only for the driver to immediately order him to shut the window. He did so, only for David to look back as they drove away and see the woman holding a huge pair of shears behind her back like a pair of scissors! He recalled the driver explaining that the reason for asking for an odd amount of change was that, while you were occupied counting it out, you would be robbed at 'shear-point' as it were and all of your money taken.

So, despite the tour disappointingly not being extended to more US locations, it had been a substantial success, with sold-out attendances throughout. This is Van der Graaf Generator, though, so you don't expect a happy ending so simple surely? That's good, because there wasn't one, as it became clear when sorting out the finances that somehow, owing to a calamitous financial mishap, none of the hotels had been paid for. There was a large crew entourage, with the band having been arranged to travel in style, and the cost was such that all of the profits from the tour were instantly wiped out.

If not the last straw, this was certainly a significant one for Hugh Banton, who had been feeling increasingly disillusioned with life on the road for the past year or so. Having only been married in 1975, it was a bad time for constant band work to suddenly begin happening, and he was feeling it to be very wearing. He returned alone from New York, and had by then made his decision to leave the band, which – in traditional Van der Graaf Generator fashion – he announced by way of a letter to his three bandmates. It was nothing if not amicable, however, and he agreed to stay on until the end of the year to fulfil existing commitments to tour the UK and France. As Hugh says about the time now:

Things had just come to a head, really. The thing is – and this is as true today as it always was – that for most of the time being in a rock band and touring is a rather tedious life! The shows themselves are great, and the daytime stuff can be fun as well at times, but so much of it is just waiting around for things to happen, and endless travelling, and I'd really just had enough of it in 1976. I'd just got married and I wanted to spend more time at home, so I just thought I'd much rather go back to my other job of doing the electronics side of things. In fact, I worked it out recently, and I think my time over the years has been split at about 70 per cent doing electronics and 30 per cent playing music!

The UK tour was, by contrast to Canada, a rather depressing experience, with venues often poorly attended and the band emotionally weary. The same downbeat atmosphere was present during the shows in France in December, until Hugh played his last show (of the 1970s) with Van der Graaf Generator, at a single German show in Saarbrücken. A poignant affair, the support band for the show were actually called 'Farewell', and David Jackson claims to have kept the backstage pass laminate reading, appropriately, 'Farewell Van der Graaf Generator'.

Back in the UK, the final farewell scene between Hugh and the band was less *Brief Encounter* and more 'politely English', as they let him out of the car in Manchester for him to get the train down to London. He got out of the car, they all said goodbye... and that was that. As Hugh said later, 'It was an awkward moment.'

Van der Graaf would regroup and continue in the new year, but in a very different form and certainly would be a very different entity indeed.

1977 – Still Possessed By The Promise Of The Pleasure Dome

The Quiet Zone / The Pleasure Dome
Personnel:
Peter Hammill: vocals, piano, electric and acoustic guitars
Graham Smith: violin
Nic Potter: bass
Guy Evans: drums and percussion
David Jackson: saxophone on 'The Sphinx In The Face' and 'The Sphinx Returns'
Recorded at Foel, Morgan and Rockfield Studios, May–June 1977
Produced by Peter Hammill
Released: 2 September 1977 (UK: Charisma, US: Mercury)
Highest chart places: Did not chart
Running time: 43:34
Tracklisting:
1. 'Lizard Play' (Hammill) 4.29, 2. 'The Habit Of The Broken Heart' (Hammill) 4.40, 3. 'The Siren Song' (Hammill) 6.05, 4. 'Last Frame' (Hammill) 6.15, 5. 'The Wave' (Hammill) 3.15, 6. 'Cat's Eye/Yellow Fever (Running)' (Hammill, Smith) 5.21, 7. The Sphinx In The Face (Hammill) 5.59, 8. 'Chemical World' (Hammill) 6.12, 9. 'The Sphinx Returns' (Hammill) 1.18

Over (Peter Hammill)
Personnel:
Peter Hammill: vocals, piano, guitar, synthesizer, organ
Nic Potter: bass
Graham Smith: violin
Guy Evans: drums and percussion
Recorded at Foel and Rockfield Studios, June–July 1976
Produced by Peter Hammill
Released: April 1977
Highest chart places: Did not chart
Running time: 46:51
All songs written by Peter Hammill
Tracklisting:
1. 'Crying Wolf' 5.13, 2. 'Autumn' 4.18, 3. 'Time Heals' 8.44, 4. 'Alice (Letting Go)' 5.40, 5. 'This Side Of The Looking Glass' 7.00, 6. 'Betrayed' 4.45, 7. '(On Tuesdays She Used To Do) Yoga' 3.57, 8. 'Lost And Found' 7.14

It was clear at the beginning of 1977 that there would have to be significant changes. Hugh Banton's departure had left a considerable hole, and what was more, it was not one which was about to be filled in the obvious way. Guy Evans has said that neither Peter Hammill nor he considered drafting in another keyboard player, even for a moment. 'Hugh Banton was the organist in Van der Graaf Generator, and that was that,' as he put it. That is an attitude which demonstrated significant loyalty and also respect for their departed bandmate, but also led to something of a conundrum. Firstly, what would they use to replace the organ in the sound, but secondly, Hugh's absence also removed the bass via his pedals, so there needed to be two elements addressed.

The bass situation was quite logically, if perhaps unexpectedly, fixed, as Nic Potter was brought back into the fold for the first time since he quit back in 1970. He had still remained in the Van der Graaf orbit, appearing on solo albums and *The Long Hello* project, and most recently having played on Hammill's still-to-be-released record *Over*, and he was in a position whereby he was happy to step in and give it another go. It was some nice continuity for the fans as well, of course, which never goes amiss.

The rest of the gap in the sound was trickier, however, as it was needing to be not only a question of who would come in, but also what instrument. At this point, it was very much Peter and Guy driving the recruitment, as David Jackson was rather preoccupied with his home life, with the baby being still very young, so he, by his own admission, did not contribute too much to the situation, understandably. As it happened, the answer to the recruitment issue was found in yet another labelmate from the Charisma stable – which, more than most labels in the 1970s, does appear to have had very much of a 'family' feel to it – as Graham Smith, from the recently split band String Driven Thing was brought in to see how things went at rehearsals. In complete contrast to anything the band had incorporated previously, Graham was an electric violinist.

Graham Smith was somewhat older than the rest of the band – having been born in 1941, he was already in his late thirties, and a veteran of not only rock music, but a distinguished classical career. Encouraged to take up violin by his father, the gifted Graham began playing in public aged seven, and at the age of 12, was awarded a junior scholarship to the Royal Academy Of Music. From there, he joined the Halle Orchestra, before moving up to Scotland and first to the BBC Scottish Symphony Orchestra, before becoming assistant leader of the Scottish National Orchestra in his late twenties. It was at this point, as the 1970s loomed into view, that rock music (and in particular the likes of Black Sabbath, The Moody Blues and Pink Floyd) entered his focus for the first time, and belatedly challenged Beethoven to roll over and tell Tchaikovsky the news. After playing for a while in a band named Chiccona, he joined the formative, and much more interesting String Driven Thing, who soon joined the Charisma roster, playing on some of the multi-act package shows with the likes of Van der Graaf, Genesis and Lindisfarne. By this point, as Smith puts it, he had undergone 'a bit of late teenage rebellion, in my mid-thirties – long overdue!' and fully embraced the rock and roll 'dark side' of the musical force. Following the split of String Driven Thing in 1976, he stayed on as a sort of in-house Charisma session musician, playing on albums by Steve Hackett among others, and most recently had also appeared on Hammill's *Over* recordings. Thus the new five-piece Van der Graaf Generator began rehearsals in late January 1977.

Graham Smith was immediately proving to be a good addition to the ranks, as his unorthodox, highly amplified and distinctive violin playing bore resemblance to both David Jackson's sax and also Hugh Banton's keyboards in different ways, being able to lay down a spiky, aggressive lead contribution or a more chordal, sometimes almost ambient backing in others, with a lot of scope for light and shade. That was the good news. The bad news was that within a few days, the band suffered another blow, when Jackson followed Hugh Banton's lead by resigning himself. He had already been finding it difficult to fully engage or commit 100 per cent as he previously had, with his young family, but he was also extremely worried about the financial security. Following the Italian truck disaster and also the loss of the Canadian profits over the hotel booking oversight, he was understandably uneasy about how regular the income from the band might be, and acutely aware of the need to put food on the table and pay the mortgage. He has also said that he wasn't feeling the band was quite the same without Hugh's presence, and was less than convinced by the new instrumental direction, so he elected to take his leave. As he said himself in a 1990 interview with Mick Dillingham:

We spent a week rehearsing, but I found the situation insurmountable. I just couldn't see how it could work. At the end of that week, I resigned. I thought if I left now, it would help the reformation; me being there with a broken heart would not help it. My spirit had gone, the two years and all the problems had wiped it away. I didn't want to be away from home. I had a little baby, and nine months spent touring that year didn't seem to be a thing I wanted to do.

Suddenly, the line-up was looking a lot leaner, with a big chunk of the sound gone, and the Van der Graaf 'core' was now very much Hammill and Evans, as the hub around which the band revolved.

Undeterred, the band persevered as a four-piece, honing their sound into a more stripped-back and punchy entity, with Peter Hammill having said that he wanted to capture some of the punk energy and spirit of the time, and hitch it to some slightly more sophisticated music. Most prog rock bands attempting this at the time would have been looking at almost certain ridicule and flat-on-their-face failure, but then again, VdGG had always had the backing of several within the new wave scene for their own attitude and sometimes belligerent defiance in the face of compromise. Put simply, they could carry off a reinvention which the likes of Pink Floyd or Yes simply would not have been able to do.

The band kept rehearsing for the next month before making their live debut at The Roundhouse on 20 February. The show was a sold-out success, with Potter and Smith bowled over by the experience; Potter admitted that he hadn't realised how big the band had become in his absence, while Smith was revelling in the luxury of finally being the headliner in such a venue, rather than warming the crowd up for the main attraction (which would often have actually been Van der Graaf!). March brought a trip to Belgium and Holland – as well as, for the first time, up to Scandinavia with shows in Sweden and Norway. Guy Evans was quoted in *The Book* as saying how incredibly cold it was in Norway: he stepped outside the hotel on one occasion only to hear a crashing sound and finding it was an ice-breaking ship making its way up the nearby river, and he also went for a walk at night and found Nic Potter stuck, as he had gone out in a light jacket and his hand had frozen to a doorknob in the minus 25-degree temperature!

Evans himself was going to drive the band and some gear, and to that end, they had to get a hire car. They would have wanted a very large one considering they had guitars, amps and suitcases to transport. Unfortunately, they got a Ford Escort, which necessitated around half an hour of 3D geometry just to fit the gear and the four humans into the car, with just about every spare cubic inch at a premium. There were also no chains on the tyres with which to take on the completely iced-up roads, and so this small vehicle crammed to the roof with limbs and equipment made its way, as he put it, 'fish-tailing and skidding'. Miraculously, they survived in one piece.

From 14 March, Van der Graaf played a week of shows with Hawkwind in Germany, a double bill which must have been quite something. Hawkwind were undergoing a similar sea change in personnel and style since the departure of the talismanic Lemmy among others, and the shifting of emphasis from the fantasy space-rock of albums such as *Hall Of The Mountain Grill* and *Warrior On The Edge Of Time* to 1977's much more angular and scientific *Quark, Strangeness And Charm*. In many ways, they were in the same small group of bands who could adapt to the times, as Graham Smith alluded to in an interview with Hawkwind website *Starfarer* some years later:

Van der Graaf and Hawkwind were obviously very different bands in style. Where Hawkwind had this one riff that went on and on – eventually evolving into a kind of soundscape – Van der Graaf had one riff, and another, and another – this complex musical structure. But in terms of the noise, the rawness and the energy levels during their performances, they weren't that far away. The anarchic element, and the sonic quality and rawness of punk, was there, both in the performances and sounds of Hawkwind and Van der Graaf.

Following that German tour and the odd UK show (including an unlikely support slot from folk singer/raconteur Richard Digance), Peter Hammill's solo album *Over* was finally released almost a year after it was recorded. A resolutely downbeat yet cathartic set of songs directly inspired by the departure of Alice, the album is, for those in the right frame of mind to listen, a remarkable one. Rarely can a musician have laid his soul more bare on record than this, and it makes for a powerful listening experience. Songs such as the utterly despairing 'This Side Of The Looking Glass' are dark even by the standards of Peter Hammill, but all the better and more effective for it:

I'm lost, I'm dumb, I'm blind,
I am drunk with sadness, Sunk by madness,
The wave overwhelms me, The mirror repels me,
The echo of your laugh drifts through the looking-glass
And I am alone.

Before ending with:

> The stars in their constellations,
> Each one just sadly flickers and falls…
> Without you, they mean nothing at all.

Elsewhere are titles such as 'Betrayed', 'Lost And Found' and '(On Tuesdays She Used To Do) Yoga', picking over each shred of the shattered relationship to exorcise the demons. This is absolutely not music to sing along to while doing the gardening, that much can be made absolutely clear. Those willing to travel the lonely road with Hammill, however, will find it an enriching one. The cover photo shows Peter sitting on a windowsill, the sunlight outside and the darkness inside with him. Meurglys III leans against the other side of the window, his only companion. The original title was to have been *Over My Shoulder*, with a cover depicting him appropriately looking backwards, but he felt (correctly, I believe) that *Over* was more succinct, and he also said it had the double meaning of 'It's over' or 'Get over it'. In fact, a small number of copies were released in France with *Over My Shoulder* as the title before being withdrawn.

Another radio session was done by Peter and Graham Smith, playing two songs from *Over* ('Betrayed' and 'Autumn'), together with an unexpected performance of 'Afterwards', from *The Aerosol Grey Machine* way back in 1969. In May, however, it was time for the big event: the recording of a new album with the much-reconstructed band, and although there was some work done at Morgan and Rockfield, most was done in the familiar (at least to Peter and Guy) surroundings of Foel Studios once again, with Ian Gomm and Dave Anderson back in the control room. The recording was completed in around a month – again, a quick turnaround – though it wouldn't be released until September, under the title of *The Quiet Zone / The Pleasure Dome*. The material was definitely leaner and more concise in general than the sound of old, but still far from straightforward in its construction, with Graham Smith doing an admirable job throughout in terms of filling the sonic void left by Banton and Jackson. Peter Hammill also addresses the lack of a chordal instrument since Hugh's departure by contributing far more electric guitar than he had ever done before, while Nic Potter's bass sound is immense. The album, when it was released in September, would be credited to the shorter name of simply Van der Graaf, with that truncated form having been adopted officially, although gig listings and even Charisma PR material often continued to append the Generator. Guy Evans says about this name change: 'It was to differentiate this version of the band as a separate musical entity in one sense, but it was also a reaction to the fact that things had become 'leaner and meaner' in the music scene generally, and the punchier name seemed to suit the time better in a way.'

In July came the earlier-mentioned BBC recording with John Lydon (or 'Rotten' as he still was) eulogising in an interview about his love for Van der Graaf in general and Hammill in particular, which would have done the band no harm at all in terms of contemporary kudos, clearly. Following that, however, they headed over to Ibiza to headline a festival there, called the 'Primo Festival di Musica Popula', which ultimately turned into two shows, with chaotic and almost fatally disastrous results.

The first show at the festival went off extremely well. The band played an excellent set and went down the proverbial storm. Having decided to spend ten days over there, combining a holiday with the appearance, they accepted the opportunity to play a second show around five days later at the same venue. This proved to be a mistake, as everything which had gone right the first time went unerringly wrong on the second occasion.

The venue was a bullring, with the band's dressing room being the matadors' room. On the afternoon of the show, at the soundcheck, Guy Evans sustained a nasty injury which rendered him unconscious when he walked up onto the stage and struck his head hard on the end of a horizontal piece of scaffolding. On coming to, he remembers being in the bullring's chapel, lying on a concrete slab surrounded by nuns, which must surely have been an alarming thing to wake up to. It was, he has said, where they would bring the matadors who had been gored by the bulls, where they would have the last rites administered. Not the ideal preparation for a show in the evening, one would think. His recollection of the show itself becomes even more bizarre, as the band apparently walked out only to see a line of stony-faced women sitting in front of them on the edge of the stage, for no reason that they could ascertain. The actual show he could only describe as 'demonic' in its intensity. Nic Potter played at a fearsome level of volume and distortion at times, and indeed after the show he immediately apologised, as he swore that his sound levels kept going up and down of their own accord in alarming fashion, despite his not touching any settings. Graham Smith apparently got into this same zone of being on the edge of chaos, and the band were all feeling rather shaken by the end.

The following day, still a little jumpy, they went to the beach to relax, going into the sea to help to 'chill out' (as they say in Ibiza these days, of course). Graham Smith was particularly enjoying the surf which was coming up, with Evans again not far behind him. Suddenly, however, a powerful undertow could be felt, and Guy immediately called for everyone to get back to the safety of the beach. Graham either failed to hear him or was simply enjoying himself, when he was suddenly pulled out to deep water, visibly panicking. Guy at first made to strike out after him to help but, realising that he wouldn't be able to get back if he reached him, had to make the split-second decision to leave his bandmate and head back for help. It was as well that he did as, despite being a good swimmer himself, and being adept enough to use techniques such as swimming parallel to the shore until the rip tide went the right way, he became exhausted with the force of the current, and seriously doubted whether he would make it back. He did get back to the shore, arriving exhausted and urging people to get together and perhaps form a chain to go out to try and rescue Graham. In the very nick of time, however, someone reached the stricken Smith with an inflatable lilo, which he managed to just about scramble onto before blacking out. Nic Potter recalled that when he was brought back to the beach, he was unconscious, and they seriously feared that he might actually be dead, but fortunately, a doctor was on hand to provide emergency first aid, and he was brought round.

Clearly, by this time, all concerned were in a highly agitated state, but before they left the beach, Guy made the suggestion that in order to 'get back on the horse' as the saying goes, and overcome any lingering fear, they should go back into the shallows and stand in the water, to get the feel of it again in a safer environment. This was agreed upon, as he recalled in *The Book*: 'We did just that, and my daughter Tamra was with me. She was about seven at the time. She was behind me, and the water depth wasn't even up to my knees. Suddenly I heard her cry and turned around just to see her disappearing! The seabed had just given way beneath her, and I reached down and pulled her up. So then it was out of the water!'

This wasn't the end of the unsettling events surrounding this trip, however, as the following day Guy and his daughter were invited by the couple who had done the catering for the show to visit them at their farmhouse on the other side of the island. They were invited to stay for a party further up in the hills that evening, and so Guy headed back to collect some evening clothes to change into. When he was approaching the house again on his return with the change of clothes, he was startled and unnerved to see what he could only describe as appearing to be some kind of UFO – a bright, glowing and enormous object (he estimated it must have been around 50,000 feet up), which hovered for a while before flying off at tremendous speed to the west. He was wondering whether he had imagined it, when he arrived to find everyone outside the house and watching the sky themselves, having seen the same thing. Not only that, but Nic Potter reported seeing exactly the same phenomenon from the band's base on the other side of the island, and even said that everyone in the village where they were staying were outside, talking about the inexplicable sight.

The next day they flew back, glad to be away from such a seemingly cursed week, but the *X-Files* activity didn't stop there, apparently following them back to the UK. Guy Evans took his daughter to visit his girlfriend back home, and when he went to pick her up again, things got even stranger, as he reported in *The Book*:

> So I got in my car to go and pick her up, turned on the ignition, and the whole of the ignition system just carbonised… it caught fire and was just toast. So I got on my bike and went over there. When I was there, I borrowed my friend's car, got into that, turned on the ignition and the same thing happened! I was absolutely, unbelievably creeped out. So I got into car number three, and the dashboard disintegrated. It just fell out and was not usable. Something was just out of whack and I've never, ever been able to explain it…

Nic Potter confirmed that there was a lot of strange activity going on, and has suggested that it almost went as far as breaking the band up. He tied it in a loose way to the intensity and almost dangerous power of the way that particular line-up played, with Graham Smith talking years later to *Mojo* magazine about an 'atmosphere' which followed the band around, and that they felt extremely anxious at times.

****

Partly to anchor the band musically to a greater structural base, and make the whole playing experience less chaotic and prone to extremes of triumph or disaster at any moment, it was decided to expand to a five-piece and bring in another instrument. Given that they had lost an organist and a sax and flute player, and were relying for guitar on Peter Hammill's intense yet untamed playing, and that they had brought in bass guitar and violin, there could have been several different instruments that they might have been expected to draft in. The one they went for would not have been at the top of too many people's lists of suggestions: with the arrival of Charles Dickie in August, Van der Graaf now included a cello.

In fact, Dickie played keyboards too, and would move from one to another in live shows, but his primary instrument for which he was brought in was the cello. It was felt that it would go with the violin to form the world's most unconventional string section, and serve to provide a stable base to the music, as well as softening the edges when required. The really odd thing was that, from being left as a band without any strings after Potter left in 1970, with the exception of the drums and any time Peter or Charles played piano, Van der Graaf had gone entirely the other way and were ALL strings. The fact that they retained as much of their recognisable style as they did speaks volumes about the unique quality and adaptability of the music, as well as the strength of Hammill and Evans on their own contributions. One wonders how recognisable Tangerine Dream or Kraftwerk would have remained had they suddenly discarded the electronics and taken up guitars, violins and cellos instead...

The new man, Charles Dickie, was born in 1949 in South London. Another childhood classical musician like Smith, he began by playing piano before he took up the cello at age 13. Like Smith, he had something of a rock epiphany, in his case, from seeing Eric Clapton with John Mayall's Bluesbreakers at the Marquee in the mid-1960s. He was so inspired by Clapton's ability to improvise his solos on the spot without any of the sheet music he had grown up with himself, that he immediately went home and began experimenting with long, improvised solos on the cello or the piano – extended cello soloing must surely be a niche element even within the environment we are covering on these pages! In fact, going on to watch the likes of Hendrix and Cream play over the next couple of years (being particularly impressed by Jack Bruce, with the cello having similarities as a four-stringed bass instrument) led him to experiment more and more, even perfecting the use of such guitar-oriented techniques as pinch harmonics on the cello strings, and could make the instrument sound more like Hendrix than anyone could have a right to expect.

After attending music college (and stepping back into the classical music of his background), be began playing in different bands, including a London-based blues outfit he founded himself, oddly named The Chas Saxe-Coburg Blues Band. When the invitation to join Van der Graaf came along, he jumped at it, and remembers a testing audition process during which he had to improvise with the band on cello and then piano, for about half an hour each, followed by him being asked to put a cello part on to a piece from the *Quiet Zone* album, from one single hearing. When he joined, he made quite a remarkable sound with Graham Smith, as both were playing their instruments in a rather idiosyncratic way. Smith, for his part, rather than using a standard electric violin, instead used a traditional acoustic instrument, amplified with an attached pickup, also using effects such as the wah-wah pedal, and combined with Dickie's unusual playing techniques on an amplified cello made for yet another Van der Graaf sound element like no other.

As Charles was settling into the band, however, the album which they had recorded just before his arrival was released, on 2 September. Titled *The Quiet Zone / The Pleasure Dome*, it was nominally split into two sides with those titles, the first being *The Quiet Zone*. Even the cover was split into two, with the front being an illustration of an acrobat on a trapeze in orbit over a planet and titled as *The Quiet Zone*. Flip it over to the reverse, however, and there was another alternate cover image titled *The Pleasure Dome*; this one being a rather odd photograph of the four members. Potter and Evans are only just visible at the sides, in profile, with Hammill and Smith taking centre stage. Hammill, in a white jacket and tie, is tossing a silver apple in the air with an expression of wonder, while Smith, next to him, is playing the violin in a dinner jacket and bow tie, with an expression suggesting that either he really doesn't want to be there or something (perhaps levitating silver fruit) is irritating him rather strongly. Depending on when precisely the photo was taken, the fact that he is wearing a 'dickie bow' may be significant.

The album is very impressive in places, but overall is something of a mixed bag. The division of the material into the two themed sides seems somewhat arbitrary – in general, the more upbeat material is on *The Pleasure Dome*, but far from exclusively. Strong highlights are the opening 'Lizard Play', the sophistication of 'The Siren Song', the dramatic 'Last Frame' (stuffed with sinister photographic imagery) and perhaps the album highlight, the propulsive and energetic 'Cat's Eye / Yellow Fever (Running)'. This last-named song is the only one not a solo Hammill composition, being an adaptation-cum-rewrite of a piece of Graham Smith music which he had written before joining the band. With the urgent, staccato violin and bass driving the music along, Hammill's voice is equally vibrant, with the whole effect being perhaps closest to the idea of the punk attitude with the compositional depth. 'The Sphinx In The Face', another heavy and dynamic track, features a guest appearance from David Jackson on sax, and suffers only from a rather irritating chorus, repeated for some time after the music dies away behind it at the end; this has been the subject of some fan disagreement, in the same way as the extended coda to 'Meurglys III' on the previous album. The short reprise at the close of the album, 'The Sphinx Returns', fades in again with that same chorus, and doesn't tend to be anyone's favourite moment on the record!

Nothing on the album is poor, but the other three tracks, 'Wave', 'Chemical World' and 'The Habit Of The Broken Heart' are less memorable, with 'Wave' actually working better as an instrumental demo which was included on CD releases of the album. Note that the 'habit' of the broken heart actually refers to nuns, in another Hammill swipe at the subject of Catholicism and religion. There were two other tracks recorded which were added to CD reissues: 'Door' is a heavy rocking track which would appear on the following year's *Vital* live album, as would the equally powerful but more notable 'Ship Of Fools', which was the B-side of the 'Cat's Eye' single. Charles Dickie appears on this recording, his first and last studio release with Van der Graaf, but his contribution is stronger still on the later live version.

Guy Evans today speaks very fondly of the four-piece line-up, with the edginess and excitement that it engendered, as he told me:

It was very spiky and aggressive, and I think that there was a feeling that we wanted to soften it and smooth things out a little by getting Charles in with the cello, but I'm not sure we ever really quite got there. Looking back now, I think the four-piece is my favourite of those line-ups, just because of the feeling we had of being right out there on the edge. I'm not sure I necessarily felt like that at the time, but certainly, looking back, there was a unique quality there.

Some sources have claimed that Charles Dickie played his first gig with the band in Amsterdam on 5 October, but recollections of band members indicate that he actually played two outdoor festivals with them on 3 and 4 October before that. These two festivals featured various levels of disaster, which anyone having reached this point in the story will not be surprised by. The first, however, in Germany, must be singled out as the most shambolically mismanaged festival ever staged – or partially staged in this case.

The event was the Scheessel First Rider Open Air Festival which took place in Hamburg on the weekend of 3 and 4 October or should have. There had been a similar event there in 1973, which had lasted three days and been a roaring success, so hopes were high among those in attendance. They shouldn't have been. A biker-related event, it took the decision to hire Hells Angels as security for the event – presumably because the similar arrangement at Altamont in 1969 had gone down so well, with just the one murder taking place as the Rolling Stones performed. To make things even worse, two groups of Angels were recruited but were told on the day that only one of the contracts would be honoured and paid, which would not be the most auspicious start to proceedings. The line-up, however, was an impressive one, with some 22 bands announced to be playing, from Steppenwolf and The Byrds, through Camel, Barclay James Harvest, Colosseum II, and even on to The Damned and The Stranglers, who would have made unlikely bedfellows with the above mentioned, one would think. In the event, any squabbling wasn't a problem, as only six of the bands actually turned up. In the case of some of them, such as Steppenwolf and The Byrds, this was understandable given the fact that they didn't actually exist at that time. In some other cases, in a display of breathtaking financial naivete, bands were actually paid in full before the event even took place. No one will be surprised to hear that they didn't show up. This led to a crisis as the event was clearly not going to happen, and the organiser attempted to abscond with the money.

With 30,000 fans in attendance and only a quarter of the line-up in place, astoundingly the festival began as if it was going to go ahead. Whoever the Dutch band Long Tall Ernie and the Shakers were, they opened proceedings. Camel, Colosseum II, Golden Earring and Van der Graaf also played, with German electronic artist Klaus Schulze due to go on next, when the organisers suddenly decided to announce that there were no more bands and that the event was cancelled. The fans, understandably unhappy at this, rioted. The Hells Angels, understandably unhappy at not being paid, stood aside and let them, with the result that the crowd burned the stage to the ground and also much of the backstage area. Klaus Schulze never did get to play.

The following day it was on to Rotterdam for another festival appearance at the New Pop Zuiderpark. On this occasion, there were significant delays putting back the band's start time by hours, something which Charles Dickie had never experienced. Having a drink to steady his nerves, he ended up having far too many nerve-steadiers, and by the time the band went on, he was much the worse for wear. He began playing all right, but it became clear that he had problems when he was to change from cello to piano after the first song, and he was reportedly unable to find the piano. In his defence, as an extremely professional musician, this was very much a one-off, and was accepted by the band as such – but he did later describe it as 'a harrowing experience' getting through the show.

Several other planned European shows were reportedly cancelled, but one which did take place was in Luxembourg on 11 October, for which the band once again elected to fly over. They arranged a tiny aeroplane, which they just about fitted into in rather cramped conditions (it held a maximum of six people, and there were five of them plus the pilot, so space was at a premium in this tiny craft). When they landed at the equally tiny airport at their destination, they had to ask a question rarely posed when landing in an aeroplane: namely, 'what time does the airport close?' Unfortunately, the reply was 'ten o'clock', which was the time the band were scheduled to be midway through their second set. Therefore they had to arrange, on returning after the show, for someone to come and 'open up the airport'. Indeed, it cannot be often that you have the experience of taking off only to look behind you and see the runway lights being immediately switched off again!

In October and November, the band embarked on a fairly lengthy UK tour, taking in 20 or so dates, including one on 5 November at Manchester University (where all of this began of course), which Hugh Banton came to. Since leaving the band, he had been working for an organ manufacturer based in Rochdale, so this was a local show for him and, it also being Peter Hammill's birthday, he brought him a bottle of tequila. For the tour, and with the addition of Charles Dickie to the sound, they had put in two songs never played by the old line-up, namely 'A Plague Of Lighthouse Keepers' (albeit a part of it, in a medley with 'The Sleepwalkers'), and also the desolate sci-fi hopelessness of 'Pioneers Over c'. These followed on from the equally surprising decision by the four-piece, earlier in the year, to introduce 'My Room (Waiting For Wonderland)' into their repertoire, the only track from *Still Life* never to have been played live by the old band. This UK tour saw, for the first time, a variety of stage projections and other visual effects introduced (including the expected space imagery for 'Pioneers'), at the behest of Charisma, who insisted they try to keep in step, in a more low-key way of course, with the highly visual nature of bands such as Genesis. The problem with that was that the money for these visuals was in short supply, and they were not really developed further.

The final gig of the tour, in Dunstable on 13 November, was notable for a rather bizarre decision by Peter Hammill. Because the band were flying over to France for a show the very next night in Lille, he announced that the Dunstable show would officially be the first date of the French tour, and proceeded to play the whole show wearing a beret and did all of the between-song announcements in French! This tour of France (and a couple of gigs in neighbouring countries) lasted around two weeks in total, but this was still time enough for one of the shows to be torched by a mob of political terrorists. The band were playing a show in a concrete sports hall in the town of Pau, near to the Spanish border, on 19 November, when the venue was infiltrated by a group of Basque Separatists who proceeded to pour petrol into the building and set it on fire. In what seems like a remarkably calm and orderly response, according to Charles Dickie they were told to continue playing despite the flames, so that the audience would not panic. He recalls getting up from the piano when he spotted the fires and going over to Peter Hammill to ask whether they should actually stop, only to be told, 'No, definitely not.' In the manner of the band on the *Titanic*, they continued to play, and remarkably it seems to have worked as the flames were extinguished and no one was injured.

This tour proved to be the final live work of the year, with the band amazingly taking the whole of December off, but there were plans in place for the new year. One of those plans, a tour of the USA, which had been mentioned sometime earlier in a newsletter to fans, would not come to pass, but the other intention, namely to record the first official Van der Graaf live album, most certainly would.

1978 – The Ship Of Fools Runs Aground

Vital
Personnel:
Peter Hammill: vocals, piano, guitar
Graham Smith: violin
Nic Potter: bass
Guy Evans: drums and percussion
Charles Dickie: cello, electric piano, synthesizer
David Jackson: saxophone and flute
Recorded at the Marquee, 16 Jan 1978
Produced by Guy Evans
Released: July 1978 (UK: Charisma, US: PVC Records)
Highest chart places: Did not chart
Running time: 86:14
Tracklisting:
1. 'Ship Of Fools' (Hammill) 6.44, 2. 'Still Life' (Hammill) 9.44, 3. 'Last Frame' (Hammill) 9.05, 4. 'Mirror Images' (Hammill) 5.51, 5. 'Medley: A Plague Of Lighthouse Keepers / The Sleepwalkers' (Hammill, Banton, Evans, Jackson) 13.43, 6. 'Pioneers Over c' (Hammill, Jackson) 17.08, 7. 'Sci-Finance' (Hammill) 6.13, 8. 'Door' (Hammill) 5.30, 9. 'Urban / Killer / Urban' (Hammill, Banton, Judge Smith) 8.18, 10. 'Nadir's Big Chance' (Hammill) 3.59

The Future Now (Peter Hammill)
Personnel
Peter Hammill: guitars, vocals, keyboards, harmonica, electronics
David Jackson: saxophone
Graham Smith: violin
Recorded at Sofa Sound, March–April 1978
Produced by Peter Hammill
Released: September 1978
Highest chart places: Did not chart
Running time: 45:50
All songs written by Peter Hammill
Tracklisting:
1. 'Pushing Thirty' 4.21, 2. 'The Second Hand' 3.29, 3. 'Trappings' 3.34, 4. 'The Mousetrap (Caught In)' 4.07, 5. 'Energy Vampires' 2.57, 6. 'If I Could' 4.43, 7. 'The Future Now' 4.14, 8. 'Still In The Dark' 4.41, 9. 'Mediaevil' 3.07, 10. 'A Motor-Bike In Afrika' 3.11, 11. 'The Cut' 4.21, 12. 'Palinurus (Castaway)' 4.10

The intention at the beginning of 1978 was to do something which Peter Hammill had always resisted in the past: record a Van der Graaf live album. His view had always been that a live show existed only in the memory and experience of those present, and that the soul of the event was impossible to capture on tape, or indeed, film. He still felt that way, but the truth was that recording this album – which would be a double album called *Vital* – was, indeed, absolutely vital if the group were to survive as an entity. Financial constraints, record company funding and general debt management meant that the low-cost, high-return model which a successful live recording could provide was the only practical option available. Nonetheless, Hammill was satisfied somewhat by the fact that the shows to be recorded, and hence the album itself, would include several songs as yet unreleased and, in several cases, unrecorded in the studio. This way, he argued, people were not being asked to stump up the money for a double album containing entirely songs which they already had. Not that the fans would have minded that, nor would they have been short-changed, since the Van der Graaf live experience had never been about simply reproducing a studio recording, and with the markedly different instrumentation now involved, that was more true than ever.

Two shows were arranged at the Marquee, on 15 and 16 January, with a week of rehearsals beforehand. There was to be another surprise for the fans as well, however: for the purposes of these two shows, and the resulting album, David Jackson was invited back to play with the band as a special guest – something he accepted gratefully, being very pleased by the gesture. The shows would take place over two halves, and for the second half – unbeknownst and unannounced to even the audience – he would play for the entire second part. For that half of the shows, Van der Graaf would, for the only time ever, perform as a six-piece. Rehearsals were not able to start until 8 January, however, with the first show on the 15th, so to get the rehearsal work done within a week required some serious effort – and it is probable that only four days saw work being done, with one day being spent at EAR studios in Ealing, two more at Silver Studios and a further one, on the eve of the shows, at Virtual Earth Studios.

Nowhere was that effort manifested more than with David Jackson. Although only playing half of the show, he had never played with Smith or Dickie before, was unfamiliar with any of the new arrangements and, to cap it off, was required to play on two songs which he would never even have heard before, let alone performed – as they were as yet unrecorded in the studio. To add to that, he was unable to get time off his job, which now involved him driving a 40-ton heavy goods vehicle delivering produce to supermarkets. He has described the week leading up to those shows as the most tiring of his life, as he was having to get up each morning at 4 am, do an eight-to-ten-hour shift in the truck, and then travel into London for the evening's work. A punishing schedule for sure, but it has to be said an excellent decision to get him into the band for the shows; not only tipping the hat to his contributions over the years, but also as a significant 'pull' for fans of the band to want to get hold of the album when it appeared. Firstly, however, they needed to get the recordings done, and that proved much trickier than might have been expected (though, of course, this being Van der Graaf, maybe it wouldn't be a tremendous surprise!).

The purse strings at Charisma at this point were stretched to their limit – which wasn't all that elastic at the time in any case, to be honest – and the band themselves were heavily in debt. The Static Enterprises company they had set up with Gordian a few years previously to handle financial affairs had gone bust, so they had to revert to the company Peter had set up with Gordian in 1973, Panel Enterprises. Hiring of a mobile recording unit was out of the question, but thankfully they were able to get the use of a 24-track unit owned by Yes but which was run by two old university friends of Guy, Brian Gaylor and Mike Dunne. Guy managing to borrow this unit was a lifesaver, but there were still significant problems to overcome. For the first show, there was trouble getting the recording working properly, and also reportedly, the onstage sound had some issues that night as well, so it was all down to the second show to record everything. At the soundcheck in the late afternoon, with all setup and seemingly working, they did a sample recording, only to find another unforeseen problem rearing its head. Incredibly as it may sound, so tight was the financial situation that, even though they had managed to borrow the recording gear, they were unable to raise the funds for new 24-track tapes to record on to, so they were forced to use pre-used tape with something already recorded on to it. On listening to the test recordings, they discovered that, owing to the levels of the previous content of the tapes, there was too much sound bleeding over from those recordings, and in order to be usable, the tapes would have to be professionally erased. Thus, with the crowd already lining up outside the venue waiting for the doors to open, Guy had to run over to the nearby Trident Studios, tapes under his arm, to get them put through one of Trident's erasers. Except that, this being Van der Graaf, Trident Studios were completely out of action with refurbishments, so – with the queue getting longer all the time – a taxi was called to get over to Air Studios in nearby Oxford Street to get them erased there. Obviously, with not only the recording media but also a band member being held up, the show was having to be delayed.

Finally, things were able to get underway, with Mike Dunne as recording engineer, and the show was recorded. The setlist for the night was 'Cat's Eye / Yellow Fever' and 'The Sphinx In The Face' opening the show, then 'Ship Of Fools', 'Still Life', 'Last Frame' and 'Door' closing the first half of the show. With David Jackson then joining the band, they tackled a new song 'Mirror Images' before going back into the past for a 13-minute medley of 'A Plague Of Lighthouse Keepers' and 'The Sleepwalkers' followed by a 17-minute rendition of 'Pioneers Over c' and another new song, 'Sci-Finance' before a performance of 'Urban', with an instrumental portion of 'Killer' inserted into it. Two more encore songs were also performed, namely the Hammill solo tracks 'Nadir's Last Chance' and, according to reports, 'Crying Wolf'.

Soon after those shows, the band had planned to undertake a tour of North America, but sadly the financial situation precluded that, and with the tour cancelled, they took a short break from activity. Peter was able to take a short trip to the US himself in February, in a far less expensive solo guise, playing 14 shows across four venues in Los Angeles, San Francisco, Kansas City and New York. The first three dates, at the Troubadour in Los Angeles, saw him doing two shows each night, with his first set beginning at 9 pm and his second ending at 2am. The two dates in Kansas City were the ones at the All Souls Unitarian Church, where the performances used as the bonus tracks on the later CD releases of *Chameleon In The Shadow Of The Night* and *The Silent Corner And The Empty Stage* were recorded. Such was the cult appeal of Hammill and VdG that it has been reported that people travelled from 12 different states to attend the Kansas City shows, with them being the only dates in between the two coasts. It is the forever tragic irony of both Van der Graaf and Peter Hammill that they could attract such a devoted and passionate following without that being translated into mainstream numbers, with finances directly seeing to the band's eventual demise.

Nevertheless, Peter's trip had been successful and, following two final nights (two shows each) at a venue called The Other End in New York City, he returned home to spend the following month, across March and April, recording his next solo album. In between the Marquee shows and the US trip, he had moved to a newly rented house in West Byfleet, Surrey – and of course, his Sofa Sound home studio moved with him, with the result that the album would be recorded at 'Sofa Sound, Surrey' rather than 'Sofa Sound, Sussex'.

More than most of his recent albums. *The Future Now* would be an almost entirely homegrown affair – Graham Smith and David Jackson both appeared, but only on two tracks each, and not the same ones. The album was to comprise 12 tracks of markedly shorter duration, so it ended up with eight of the 12 being entirely solo Hammill recordings, and none with more than one other musician appearing. It could easily be seen as a provisional marker being laid in the sand for future work should VdG come to a shuddering halt – which all were only too aware at this point was a distinct risk.

While Peter was over in the US and busy recording the album, Guy Evans had the responsibility of producing and mixing the *Vital* recordings, to which end he took the tapes to Foel Studios once again and settled in with Dave Anderson as his assistant in the work. Almost as soon as the work began, problems reared their head. There was an early setback as some work had to be abandoned and restarted following the vocals being mixed out of phase (Guy, by his own admission, was still in some ways honing his sound engineering craft, and mistakes were a part of the learning process), but the biggest technical hurdle came with David Jackson's sax parts, which were poorly recorded almost to the point of being unusable before some audio wizardry from Guy made the day safe. David, in his 1990 interview with Mick Dillingham, said:

> They dropped the 'Generator' at that point which was a nice gesture, and toured very successfully for 18 months or so as Van der Graaf. They put out one album, *The Quiet Zone/The Pleasure Dome,* which is excellent. I was working as a driver when I got a call from them to guest at two Marquee gigs to be recorded as a live album, and by this time they had brought in Charles Dickie on cello. The finished album, *Vital,* is a personal disaster for me, I can't bear to hear it. Usually I would have wanted four tracks of the 24-track mobile they set up, two because of the stereo nature of my saxophone set-up and two for the effects pedal etc. on each channel. What I got was one track – worse still, when Guy Evans came to mix the tapes, he found that the mobile had been faulty and there was just total silence on my track. What he had to do was go through the other tracks looking for where my sax would have bled onto

a track, like the vocal track, and then take out my sax and boost it up and clean it – and that's what you hear on the record.

While Guy has disputed the accuracy of this, stating that the sax had been recorded, he said that it was accompanied by a loud and very obtrusive buzzing which had to be carefully equalised out – a long and painstaking process.

Whatever the truth of the matter, one would, in actual fact, scarcely notice if not informed of the problems, so it has to be said that the saxophone rescue mission was an excellent success.

****

With the tricky sonic wizardry done and awaiting the release of the record, May brought with it the start of another bout of touring – which in this case would turn out to be the last, at least for this iteration of the band, and for a very long time. It was clear that things were far from right financially, and Gordian Troeller was having to bear the brunt of much of this situation. Having officially stepped down from his position as the band's manager following the Marquee shows, Gordian was persuaded to come back into the fold one more time, though by this time, he was having to use his own company for the financial affairs, with Panel Enterprises having gone down the same liquidation plughole as had Static sometime earlier. He told of several difficult meetings wherein he had to go to see creditors and explain as best he could why they simply couldn't be paid for a while.

Still, the live show went on, and the band began a final leg of UK shows in St Albans on 13 May. Scarcely a tour, there were only four shows scheduled, with one of those (in Bradford on the 14th) being cancelled anyway. The final two shows were at Liverpool Eric's Club on 15 May and in Bangor on the following night. The Liverpool show at Eric's was significant in illustrating the band's success in straddling the prog/punk chasm which had threatened to engulf so many other bands, as Eric's was well known for being one of the premier punk/new wave venues in the country, and Van der Graaf being happily accepted there was, at the time, quite remarkable in its own way. By this time, Peter Hammill had grown a full beard which he planned to partly shave for the cover of *The Future Now*, which would have him staring from the front with half of his face bearded and the other half clean-shaven. He actually did the shave after the Liverpool show, leading to Graham Smith, seemingly the only man unaware of these plans in the band circle, seeing him at breakfast the next morning and fearing he had finally lost his mind! In fact, he actually played the show in Bangor with the half beard, and has said since that, despite the many distinctive fashion appearances he has adopted over the years, he has never had more comments or baffled looks before or since that semi-shaven interlude!

The dates of 18–31 May saw a final two-week trip around France, with some 13 shows being played, before two final UK shows at the Marquee again in June. After a quick trip over to Canada by Hammill for two more solo shows (was the man never still?), Van der Graaf made their final appearance as a five-piece, and in any form until the next century, at the Kohfidisch Open Air Festival in Austria, on 17 June. This was actually filmed, and was broadcast on Austrian TV on 1 July, by which time Van der Graaf had ceased to exist.

While nobody knew for certain that they were going to pull the plug after that Austrian festival show, the writing had been on the wall for some time. The decision to quit, naturally, lay with Peter Hammill and Guy Evans, and the others reportedly respected that completely. Band sources all say that it had simply become too stressful living on a fiscal knife edge, with something as simple as a van breakdown and a missed gig having the potential to spell financial ruin, and the mental pressure of it was threatening to affect performances adversely, quite understandably. That planned trip to the USA for the band had been talked about again for the period following the European dates, but it was scrapped as being sadly unfeasible, and a statement was issued announcing the termination of the band and retirement of the name. Peter Hammill has also said that one of the key elements in the timing was that it was a natural window without future firm commitments which allowed them to stop, whereas had they continued, they would have entered another 18-month cycle of touring and recording under the mounting pressures, and the end had to be called.

July saw the release of *Vital,* which, in an ironic twist of 'too little, too late', Charisma reported as being the band's highest-selling album ever. It wasn't timely enough nor anything like substantial enough to rescue the matter, however, though it was no doubt very welcome in terms of paying off some of those accumulated debts. Mercury Records had pulled out of the band's distribution in the USA and, while *Vital* came out on Charisma as usual in the UK, over there it was issued on the small PVC Records label.

The album itself is a somewhat divisive one among fans, with some absolutely loving it for the raw and uncompromising spirit it undoubtedly displays, while others at the other end of the scale failing to warm to it for precisely the same reason. Others, such as myself, reside in the middle ground. Some parts of the album are without doubt more successful than others, but when it works well, it works spectacularly well. Van der Graaf, with or without the Generator, had never been a band to sugar-coat things or make their output easy for the listener, and they certainly weren't about to start now! Oddly, the first two songs performed on the night, 'Cat's Eye / Yellow Fever' and 'The Sphinx In The Face', are both omitted from the album, meaning that it opens with the third song of the set, 'Ship Of Fools'. This was in all likelihood because with only so much music able to fit onto the double vinyl, and Peter, in particular, wanting to include all of the as-yet-unreleased songs, these were arguably the easiest to do without, regardless of quality (which going on audience recordings was excellent), though it has also been claimed that the late arrival back of the erased tapes was to blame. It did, of course, ensure that the popular figure of David Jackson ended up appearing on almost three-quarters of the final release, and it undoubtedly was a sound decision to maximise his contribution to proceedings as far as the fans were concerned.

'Ship Of Fools' makes a tremendous opening to the album. Twice as long and infinitely more powerful than the studio B-side version, it demonstrates the power and sheer heaviness which this line-up could generate with ease. This is the sort of track which the VdG iteration of the band was made for. Note that Nic Potter's bass – as it is over the whole album – is astonishing, with perhaps the filthiest, most distorted tone ever captured on tape. Some (including Graham Smith, who has complained that it overpowered his violin in the mix) have claimed it is mixed too prominently, but many devotees of the album have identified it as a key component in its success. 'Still Life' is up next, a lengthy, slow and measured arrangement which again produces great power when required to. It isn't definitive, but does offer some interesting alternatives to the familiar studio keys-and-sax arrangement. 'Last Frame', the only *Quiet Zone...* track included, is again lengthier and more powerful than the studio version, and once again not necessarily better or worse, though certainly more aggressive.

The next track played was 'Door', but this is moved to later on the album, so David Jackson enters at the beginning of the second vinyl side for a new song 'Mirror Images', which would appear the following year on Hammill's solo album *PH7*. It's a decent track, though whether it deserved a position ahead of more vintage material or else another selection from *Quiet Zone* is debatable. It's also an odd one to introduce the Jaxon sax, but that is rectified straight away with a 13-minute medley of two sections of 'A Plague Of Lighthouse Keepers' along with the second half of 'The Sleepwalkers'. It could be argued that the medley approach fully satisfies no one, but by the same token, it is well done and the two parts fit together well. The jury is out regarding the whole concept of medleys, as evidenced by the reaction when Genesis have done the same thing, and the listener's preference will be important in how they react to this one. Opening the third side is another unexpected blast of nostalgia, with 'Pioneers Over c' confounding everyone's expectations by making an appearance in the set, especially at a whopping 17 minutes duration. This one actually works very well, rearranging the parts skilfully and purposely emphasising the horror and drama of the spacefarers' fate rather than the more nuanced sense of creeping dread evoked by the studio original. There is one particular part which underlines just how effective this line-up could be, as a fast section has to morph back into the slow, deliberate main theme, and somehow part of the band (Potter in particular) introduce the slow melody while the others continue in the double-tempo part, while incredibly managing to make it all sound natural and scarcely atonal in the least. It's a piece of amazing ensemble playing and arranging.

Following this, it is back to another relatively minor new piece entitled 'Sci-Finance', which would have to wait a full decade for a studio release, on Hammill's 1988 album *In A Foreign Town*. It's enjoyable enough, but when the album was reissued on a single CD, this was one of the two tracks to be omitted for space reasons, which is perhaps significant. Opening the final side, 'Door' is next up (appearing much later as a bonus track on the *Quiet Zone* deluxe CD edition), and it is again heavier than the studio equivalent, though not the greatest piece on here. It is essentially a quasi-heavy metal juggernaut of a piece, with a breathlessly fast climax coming over as slightly clumsy. Not so with the next track, however, which sees the never-studio-released 'Urban', which was performed as an encore as far back as 1975, this time with the mid-section of 'Killer' inserted as an instrumental. 'Urban' was written around the time of Peter Hammill's relocation to Sussex, and relates very much to the town/country divide, and it is an enjoyable piece, with the use of the instrumental 'Killer' an inspired idea, as the two dovetail together naturally and effectively. The return to 'Urban' at the end is rather perfunctory, however, essentially just being a couple of iterations of the central riff, and in reality, just calling the track, 'Urban'/'Killer' would have sufficed. A manic thrash through the punky 'Nadir's Big Chance' ends the album on an upbeat note, with the reported final encore of 'Crying Wolf' omitted.

The album cover was a peculiar one. The front cover image consisted of a set of models of the band members, appearing to be made from plasticine or modelling clay, and it is an unusual image, if not the most striking. The Hammill figure, for some reason, appears to have abandoned his guitar or keyboard in favour of what looks like a large stick, which is extremely odd, and the rear cover had a photo of the band on the night, which for some unfathomable purpose is in monochrome and blurred out of all recognition. The inner gatefold was a collage of band photos, with two of the main ones being different from the US release for a reason which is not explained. In truth, it isn't one of the band's greatest designs, but it did sell in quite healthy numbers – though despite Charisma claiming it to be the band's biggest-selling album, it did not repeat the chart placing of *The Least We Can Do* some eight years earlier.

So it was that midway through 1978, the ship had finally run aground. There would be no more Van der Graaf activity for around 25 years, and even the normally hyperactive Peter Hammill did not release or record any further music in the remainder of the year. As if to put a seal on the year, in December, the sad news came through that Keith Ellis, their 1969-era bassist and popular figure around band circles, had passed away in a hotel room from a heroin overdose, something which would inspire Peter Hammill to his own tribute the following year.

Van der Graaf, with or without the Generator, for now at least, were no more. The least they could do was to wave to us. And they had.

1979 And Beyond – The Final Reel

The sad passing of Keith Ellis at the end of 1978 led to one fitting
and emotional tribute paid to him, yet one which came about via an
unlikely set of circumstances. In February and March of 1979, Peter
Hammill embarked on another US tour, this time with Graham Smith
accompanying him. The tour was a hectic one, with some 24 shows in a
month, traversing the US from New York to California. On 14 March, at
the end of the tour, he was doing a radio phone-in show on KROQ Radio,
on the second of two days at The Roxy, Los Angeles. To his immense
surprise, one of the callers into the show was Deborah Ellis, Keith Ellis'
widow. They spoke on air and, while they were talking, Deborah asked
whether he might dedicate a song to Keith at some time. He agreed.

Peter was as good as his word and, when his next solo album *PH7* was
released in September of that year, it contained a song simply entitled
'Not For Keith'. A moving and entirely appropriate epitaph, the song
painted a concise picture of the good-natured Ellis:

> He'd have laughed in my face if he saw it get mournful,
> He'd pull me up short and say 'Life carries on'…

…before ending with a poignant final verse:

> The diaries we write are those that we crave for,
> We never put the P.S. at the foot of the final page
> He deserved more time, but he never was made for middle age
> Not for middle age
> Not for Keith.

Incidentally, on the subject of the *PH7* album, it is interesting to note that,
contrary to expectations, it is not his seventh solo album but in fact, his
eighth. PH7 is, of course, the perfectly neutral state on the scale between
acidity and alkalinity, and addressing the subject of the misnumbering, he
later commented that not only was it not his seventh record, but it was,
like all of his work, anything but 'neutral', so the title was purposefully
skewed in two ways at once.

The album marked the start of an astonishing two decades of solo
activity from Hammill as, between 1979 and 2004, when Van der Graaf
Generator finally reunited, he released a scarcely credible 26 studio

albums and seven live albums. Space precludes a detailed analysis of this
huge body of work, but we shall look at the highlights.

All of the other Van der Graaf alumni also went on to release more
music to a greater or lesser degree, much of it of extremely notable
quality. There were three more instalments in the *Long Hello* series, all
of which featured various configurations of Van der Graaf men. *Volume
2*, from 1981, was helmed by Guy Evans and Nic Potter, with David
Jackson playing on six of its 13 tracks, while Stuart Gordon and sometime
Hawkwind guitarist Huw Lloyd Langton also appear on three tracks each.
Then 1982 and 1983 brought Volumes Three and Four respectively, both
primarily the work of Jackson and Evans. The third volume also had Peter
Hammill appearing, while the fourth included a cast of strangeness from
the bands Mother Gong and Life of Riley.

Chris Judge Smith went on to produce quite an amount of music
during the next few decades, including several, mainly conceptual, solo
albums and several stage musicals, both as composer and librettist. Born
storyteller that he always has been, these avenues of work are of little
surprise in a way. From the other end of the Van der Graaf story, Charles
Dickie went into session work, playing on a wide number of albums,
and notably appearing on a Number 2 UK hit single, contributing an
improvised cello part to Gordon Haskell's song 'A Little Help From You',
which was the B-side to his unexpected Christmas hit 'How Wonderful
You Are' in 2001. He also returned to the field of classical music and made
a living through music teaching. In recent times he has been playing with
a six-piece folk/rock band called Sorry About Shaun. Graham Smith went
back to his classical roots but also released a number of solo albums
following a move to Iceland, which were popular in the home market. He
moved into alternative therapy, becoming a qualified reiki master, and he
also has a number of sci-fi/fantasy novels to his name. Nic Potter went on
to work regularly with Peter Hammill during the next two decades, also
releasing some solo material. He sadly passed away in 2013 after suffering
from a degenerative condition known as Pick's disease.

Hugh Banton returned largely to his technical work, in electronics
and organ design/manufacture, but he also, along with his erstwhile
colleagues in the VdGG 'classic' line-up, dropped in a few times to appear
on Peter Hammill records. He has also made guest appearances on a
number of different artists' recordings, and even recorded a classical
album of Bach's *The Goldberg Variations* in 2002. While living in the
northwest of England, he notably appeared in his local pantomime for

several years ('oh no, he didn't!', 'oh yes, he did!' etc.), something he
maintains that he thoroughly enjoyed.

David Jackson returned to music following his heavy goods vehicle
driving spell, and later took on a regular job teaching mathematics. He
also kept his hand in musically, releasing several solo albums as well as
playing with an array of other artists – including Peter Hammill. Guy Evans
did even more work with Peter than the others, notably but not limited
to being a member of his early-1980s band The K Group. He began
teaching music theory but always kept his hand in musically, including a
good amount of time spent with the experimental and fairly avant-garde
percussion ensemble Echo City.

To go through all of the 30-odd albums Peter Hammill put out between
1979 and 2004 would be a task far too detailed for this round-up, but
there were significant developments to his career which must be looked
at. Firstly, however, mention must be made of his bizarre and faintly
surreal appearance on children's TV programme *Playaway* in 1979,
on which he performed a song about Arthurian legends and the like
called 'Tintagel By The Sea', while frolicking around with a sword and
sporting an alarming outfit of red and yellow jerkin and red tights. This
is not something which fans would have foreseen to put it mildly, and
any coming across the appearance by chance may have looked back later
wondering whether they had in fact, dreamt it. Catchy song, mind you –
and it can be found online for the curious!

Back on more familiar ground, in 1981, Hammill formed the
aforementioned band The K Group, which featured Guy Evans and Nic
Potter, as well as second guitarist John Ellis – a former member of The
Vibrators who had also played with Peter Gabriel. The K Group members
all had alter-ego names, with Evans, Potter and Ellis being Brain, Mozart
and Fury respectively, for some inexplicable reason. Indeed, Evans is still
known as 'Brain' in VdGG circles today. Guess what Hammill's nickname
was? Yep, that's right. He was K, thus explaining his 1982 album, and the
first recorded with the group, being titled *Enter K*. The origin of the 'K'
name, for man or group, is a little fuzzy, but Peter did write, somewhat
obscurely, in his website notes on the album that 'Graham Smith gave me
the name… the prophet of unlikely ventures; the constant unknown',
which in all likelihood clarifies nothing. It should also be mentioned that
the works of Franz Kafka include two characters called, firstly 'Josef K'
(*The Trial*) and also, simply 'K' (*The Castle*), but that may be the most
scarlet of red herrings! In any rate, the albums *Enter K* and *Patience*,

which were recorded with the group, are his most 'rock band'-sounding efforts for some years, while the live double album *The Margin* was perhaps the closest that fans were going to get to a Van der Graaf sound in that decade, with a thrilling version of the 20-minute epic 'Flight' (from the album *A Black Box*) being a very significant piece. Backed by Ellis, Hammill also toured as support for Marillion on their *Script* tour in 1983, performing an edgy and impressive set. At least two of the Marillion members of the time had cited Hammill as a major influence, and it seemed to be a good pairing.

Hammill's 1980s work was, following The K Group's dissolution, a little patchy, but he achieved a critical rejuvenation of sorts with the well-received and superb, 1990 album *Fish Out Of Water*. Across these two decades, he operated across a wide field bounded by avant-garde and ambient experiments on one side and acoustic prettiness on the other, with plenty of edgy and powerful straight rock and lyrical vitriol in the hinterland in between. In 1991, he finally released the incredibly long-gestating *Fall Of The House Of Usher*, which he had begun working on with Judge Smith in 1972, releasing a second, redone version in 1999. Again he traversed between the ambience of albums such as *Fireships* with much more approachable fare, and continued to follow, very resolutely, his own idiosyncratic path.

Everything changed, however, and in a way which fans could never have expected, after Peter Hammill suffered a heart attack in December 2003, two days after completing the mix of his album *Incoherence*. Taking this as a fairly plain indication of his own mortality, he was very much driven to grasp the moment while it was still available, and took the decision to scratch the 25-year-old itch and get Van der Graaf Generator back together. The 'classic' four-piece line-up, with Banton, Evans and Jackson, that is. They recorded a comeback album *Present*, and their first reunion show at the Royal Festival Hall in May 2005 (intended as possibly a one-off at the time, testing the water, so to speak) drew a crowd of 'pilgrims' from all across the globe for an evening beyond the band's wildest expectations. A full UK and European tour schedule followed, with this writer being fortunate enough to be present at a Liverpool Philharmonic show which was a spectacular success played to a packed and enraptured crowd; indeed, Guy Evans says now: 'Actually, I do remember of all the shows on that tour, the Liverpool one was especially good. The Philharmonic is a lovely venue, the sound is great and it feels very intimate with the audience despite its size.' The first show in May had been recorded and was later released as the live album *Real Time* in 2007.

After the end of the 2005 touring, however, in early 2006, a major disagreement between David Jackson and the rest of the band resulted in Jackson leaving the group, and many assumed that would be the end of the reunion, or at least that another replacement would be drafted in (Potter and Smith being touted in some quarters at the time). What few expected was that the remaining three would elect to continue as a trio, covering the sax parts between Hugh Banton's increasingly convoluted keyboard role and Peter Hammill's increased electric guitar presence. To the amazement of many doubters, this extremely difficult and risky manoeuvre paid off handsomely, with a series of trio shows in 2007 and an album, *Trisector*, the following year, silencing the naysayers decisively. In 2008 the band travelled to Japan for some shows, while in 2009, they finally managed the long-awaited North American tour, with 15 dates across the USA and also once again in Canada. Then 2011 brought another new album, *A Grounding In Numbers* and more UK and European touring, while 2012 saw a repeat visit to the USA, where the band played a headlining set at the NEARFest festival as part of the tour, as they had also done in 2009. Peter Hammill had played the festival as a solo artist in 2008, so they became almost regulars at the event around that time. It was 2012 that saw the release of the experimental and divisive avant-garde *Alt*, which featured a vocal-less VdGG improvising in the studio, to often questionable effect and much complaining from some elements of the fan base – largely because this sort of thing had been done before, on the bonus second disc of the *Present* album, but this time as a stand-alone release. If nothing else, it showed that the band were still capable of polarising the audience at this late stage in their career!

Then 2013 saw another tour of the UK and Europe, from which came a double live album entitled *Merlin Atmos*, released in 2015. This release was especially notable for live versions of both 'Flight' and, finally, the complete 'A Plague Of Lighthouse Keepers', and it is an excellent record. The quality was maintained by 2016's studio release *Do Not Disturb*, which featured some of the best new material the band had come up with for many years, and is a late-career peak without doubt – and there is even a nod back to the heady days of Italy 1972 with the song 'Alfa Berlina'. The same year also saw the release of an album of BBC sessions dating back to the early 1970s entitled *After The Flood*.

There was no new activity for some six years following this, however, as a major tour planned as a return to the road in 2020 was completely wiped out by the Covid pandemic, although many of these cancelled dates finally took place in spring 2022. The final live show played to date by the band was on 11 May 2022 in Reutlingen, Germany, with the rest of the tour being cancelled after Peter Hammill fell ill the following day en route to Nuremberg. Happily, he recovered and, at the time of writing, is reportedly on the mend.

It is remarkable to think that, considering Peter Hammill (like many other young musicians at the time) was once quoted as saying he didn't foresee himself travelling up and down the motorway at the age of 50, that the 21st-century version of the band has now been in existence for over twice as long as it was in the 1960s–1970s. Not only that, they continue to this day to provide some of the most intense and thrilling live music experiences to be found anywhere. Still 'Vital', indeed!

Appendix: The Organs of Van der Graaf Generator

Grateful thanks to Hugh Banton for supplying this detailed breakdown of the technical specifications of his various keyboard set-ups over the years:

May–August 1968 – Auditions
Organ: Thomas

Aug 1968–1969 – 'Afterwards', 'Firebrand' etc
Organ: Farfisa Compact Duo
Effects & Amps: Fluid Sound Box, Distortion box, WEM amp & speakers

1969–70 – The Aerosol Grey Machine, The Least We Can Do, H to He, BBC sessions
Organs: Farfisa Professional (also studio Hammond C3 on *H To He*)
Effects & Amps: 2 x Fluid Sound Box, Distortion box, Phasing Pedal, Hiwatt + 2x 4x12 speakers, HB Custom Leslies

1970–73 – Pawn Hearts, Chameleon…, The Silent Corner, The Long Hello
Organs: Hammond E112 inc. pedals, Farfisa Professional
Effects & Amps: 2 x Schaller Rotosound, WEM Copycat echo, Echo & organ motor switches, 3 x Distortion; 1 x Overdrive, HB Stereo spring reverb, 6 x 100W channels (Hiwatt, Radford etc.), 4 x 4x12 speakers; NP Bass speaker, 2 x WEM speakers for reverb

1975 – Godbluff, Still Life, World Record
Organ: Hammond C3 including pedals
Effects & Amps: WEM Copycat echo, Leslie, RTR speakers & Crown amps

1976 – BBC Sessions
Organ: HB1 Custom including pedals
Effects & Amps: WEM Copycat echo, 4 x 100W amp channels, 2 x RTR speakers

2004–06 – Present, Real Time Live
Organs: Roland VR-760, Roland VK-7, MIDI pedalboard
Effects & Amps: Line6 Delay Modeller, HB 6x 125W amplifiers, MIDI pedalboard, 4 main, 1 HB sub speaker, HB Custom Leslie

2007–15 – Trisector, A Grounding In Numbers, Do Not Disturb

Organs: Roland VR-760, Hammond XK3-C, MIDI pedalboard, PC running B4, FM8 etc. under Forte, HB MIDI control box

Effects & Amps: Line6 Delay Modeller, Behringer FX100, HB 6x 125W amplifiers, 4 main, 1 HB sub speaker (For the 2013 tours I replaced the Line6 Delay Modeller with a Line6 M9 Stomp Box)

2021 onward

Organs: Viscount Legend Live 2-manual, MIDI pedalboard, PC running HB3, incorporating a Touch-Screen MIDI Controller

Effects & Amps: Line6 M9 Stomp Box, HB 6x 125W amplifiers, 4 main, 1 HB sub speaker

On Track series

Allman Brothers Band – Andrew Wild 978-1-78952-252-5
Tori Amos – Lisa Torem 978-1-78952-142-9
Asia – Peter Braidis 978-1-78952-099-6
Badfinger – Robert Day-Webb 978-1-878952-176-4
Barclay James Harvest – Keith and Monica Domone 978-1-78952-067-5
The Beatles – Andrew Wild 978-1-78952-009-5
The Beatles Solo 1969-1980 – Andrew Wild 978-1-78952-030-9
Blue Oyster Cult – Jacob Holm-Lupo 978-1-78952-007-1
Blur – Matt Bishop 978-178952-164-1
Marc Bolan and T.Rex – Peter Gallagher 978-1-78952-124-5
Kate Bush – Bill Thomas 978-1-78952-097-2
Camel – Hamish Kuzminski 978-1-78952-040-8
Captain Beefheart – Opher Goodwin 978-1-78952-235-8
Caravan – Andy Boot 978-1-78952-127-6
Cardiacs – Eric Benac 978-1-78952-131-3
Nick Cave and The Bad Seeds – Dominic Sanderson 978-1-78952-240-2
Eric Clapton Solo – Andrew Wild 978-1-78952-141-2
The Clash – Nick Assirati 978-1-78952-077-4
Crosby, Stills and Nash – Andrew Wild 978-1-78952-039-2
Creedence Clearwater Revival – Tony Thompson 978-178952-237-2
The Damned – Morgan Brown 978-1-78952-136-8
Deep Purple and Rainbow 1968-79 – Steve Pilkington 978-1-78952-002-6
Dire Straits – Andrew Wild 978-1-78952-044-6
The Doors – Tony Thompson 978-1-78952-137-5
Dream Theater – Jordan Blum 978-1-78952-050-7
Electric Light Orchestra – Barry Delve 978-1-78952-152-8
Elvis Costello and The Attractions – Georg Purvis 978-1-78952-129-0
Emerson Lake and Palmer – Mike Goode 978-1-78952-000-2
Fairport Convention – Kevan Furbank 978-1-78952-051-4
Peter Gabriel – Graeme Scarfe 978-1-78952-138-2
Genesis – Stuart MacFarlane 978-1-78952-005-7
Gentle Giant – Gary Steel 978-1-78952-058-3
Gong – Kevan Furbank 978-1-78952-082-8
Hall and Oates – Ian Abrahams 978-1-78952-167-2
Hawkwind – Duncan Harris 978-1-78952-052-1
Peter Hammill – Richard Rees Jones 978-1-78952-163-4
Roy Harper – Opher Goodwin 978-1-78952-130-6
Jimi Hendrix – Emma Stott 978-1-78952-175-7
The Hollies – Andrew Darlington 978-1-78952-159-7
The Human League and The Sheffield Scene – Andrew Darlington 978-1-78952-186-3
Iron Maiden – Steve Pilkington 978-1-78952-061-3
Jefferson Airplane – Richard Butterworth 978-1-78952-143-6
Jethro Tull – Jordan Blum 978-1-78952-016-3
Elton John in the 1970s – Peter Kearns 978-1-78952-034-7
The Incredible String Band – Tim Moon 978-1-78952-107-8
Iron Maiden – Steve Pilkington 978-1-78952-061-3
Joe Jackson – Richard James 978-1-78952-189-4
Billy Joel – Lisa Torem 978-1-78952-183-2
Judas Priest – John Tucker 978-1-78952-018-7
Kansas – Kevin Cummings 978-1-78952-057-6
The Kinks – Martin Hutchinson 978-1-78952-172-6
Korn – Matt Karpe 978-1-78952-153-5
Led Zeppelin – Steve Pilkington 978-1-78952-151-1

Level 42 – Matt Philips 978-1-78952-102-3
Little Feat – Georg Purvis - 978-1-78952-168-9
Aimee Mann – Jez Rowden 978-1-78952-036-1
Joni Mitchell – Peter Kearns 978-1-78952-081-1
The Moody Blues – Geoffrey Feakes 978-1-78952-042-2
Motorhead – Duncan Harris 978-1-78952-173-3
Mike Oldfield – Ryan Yard 978-1-78952-060-6
Laura Nyro – Philip Ward 978-1-78952-182-5
Opeth – Jordan Blum 978-1-78-952-166-5
Pearl Jam – Ben L. Connor 978-1-78952-188-7
Tom Petty – Richard James 978-1-78952-128-3
Pink Floyd – Richard Butterworth 978-1-78952-242-6
Porcupine Tree – Nick Holmes 978-1-78952-144-3
Queen – Andrew Wild 978-1-78952-003-3
Radiohead – William Allen 978-1-78952-149-8
Rancid – Paul Matts 989-1-78952-187-0
Renaissance – David Detmer 978-1-78952-062-0
The Rolling Stones 1963-80 – Steve Pilkington 978-1-78952-017-0
The Smiths and Morrissey – Tommy Gunnarsson 978-1-78952-140-5
Status Quo the Frantic Four Years – Richard James 978-1-78952-160-3
Steely Dan – Jez Rowden 978-1-78952-043-9
Steve Hackett – Geoffrey Feakes 978-1-78952-098-9
Thin Lizzy – Graeme Stroud 978-1-78952-064-4
Tool – Matt Karpe 978-1-78952-234-1
Toto – Jacob Holm-Lupo 978-1-78952-019-4
U2 – Eoghan Lyng 978-1-78952-078-1
UFO – Richard James 978-1-78952-073-6
The Who – Geoffrey Feakes 978-1-78952-076-7
Roy Wood and the Move – James R Turner 978-1-78952-008-8
Stackridge – Alan Draper 978-1-78952-232-7
Van Der Graaf Generator – Dan Coffey 978-1-78952-031-6
Yes – Stephen Lambe 978-1-78952-001-9
Frank Zappa 1966 to 1979 – Eric Benac 978-1-78952-033-0
Warren Zevon – Peter Gallagher 978-1-78952-170-2
10CC – Peter Kearns 978-1-78952-054-5

Decades Series

The Bee Gees in the 1960s – Andrew Mon Hughes et al 978-1-78952-148-1
The Bee Gees in the 1970s – Andrew Mon Hughes et al 978-1-78952-179-5
Black Sabbath in the 1970s – Chris Sutton 978-1-78952-171-9
Britpop – Peter Richard Adams and Matt Pooler 978-1-78952-169-6
Phil Collins in the 1980s – Andrew Wild 978-1-78952-185-6
Alice Cooper in the 1970s – Chris Sutton 978-1-78952-104-7
Curved Air in the 1970s – Laura Shenton 978-1-78952-069-9
Donovan in the 1960s – Jeff Fitzgerald 978-1-78952-233-4
Bob Dylan in the 1980s – Don Klees 978-1-78952-157-3
Brian Eno in the 1970s – Gary Parsons 978-1-78952-239-6
Faith No More in the 1990s – Matt Karpe 978-1-78952-250-1
Fleetwood Mac in the 1970s – Andrew Wild 978-1-78952-105-4
Focus in the 1970s – Stephen Lambe 978-1-78952-079-8
Free and Bad Company in the 1970s – John Van der Kiste 978-1-78952-178-8
Genesis in the 1970s – Bill Thomas 978178952-146-7
George Harrison in the 1970s – Eoghan Lyng 978-1-78952-174-0

Kiss in the 1970s – Peter Gallagher 978-1-78952-246-4
Marillion in the 1980s – Nathaniel Webb 978-1-78952-065-1
Van Morrison in the 1970s – 978-1-78952-241-9
Mott the Hoople and Ian Hunter in the 1970s – John Van der Kiste 978-1-78-952-162-7
Pink Floyd In The 1970s – Georg Purvis 978-1-78952-072-9
Suzi Quatro in the 1970s – Darren Johnson 978-1-78952-236-5
Roxy Music in the 1970s – Dave Thompson 978-1-78952-180-1
Status Quo in the 1980s – Greg Harper 978-1-78952-244-0
Tangerine Dream in the 1970s – Stephen Palmer 978-1-78952-161-0
Tears For Fears – Paul Clark 978-178952-238-9
The Sweet in the 1970s – Darren Johnson 978-1-78952-139-9
Uriah Heep in the 1970s – Steve Pilkington 978-1-78952-103-0
Van der Graaf Generator in the 1970s – Steve Pilkington 978-1-78952-245-7
Yes in the 1980s – Stephen Lambe with David Watkinson 978-1-78952-125-2

On Screen series
Carry On... – Stephen Lambe 978-1-78952-004-0
David Cronenberg – Patrick Chapman 978-1-78952-071-2
Doctor Who: The David Tennant Years – Jamie Hailstone 978-1-78952-066-8
James Bond – Andrew Wild – 978-1-78952-010-1
Monty Python – Steve Pilkington 978-1-78952-047-7
Seinfeld Seasons 1 to 5 – Stephen Lambe 978-1-78952-012-5

Other Books
1967: A Year In Psychedelic Rock 978-1-78952-155-9
1970: A Year In Rock – John Van der Kiste 978-1-78952-147-4
1973: The Golden Year of Progressive Rock 978-1-78952-165-8
Babysitting A Band On The Rocks – G.D. Praetorius 978-1-78952-106-1
Eric Clapton Sessions – Andrew Wild 978-1-78952-177-1
Derek Taylor: For Your Radioactive Children – Andrew Darlington 978-1-78952-038-5
The Golden Road: The Recording History of The Grateful Dead – John Kilbride 978-1-78952-156-6
Iggy and The Stooges On Stage 1967-1974 – Per Nilsen 978-1-78952-101-6
Jon Anderson and the Warriors – the road to Yes – David Watkinson 978-1-78952-059-0
Misty: The Music of Johnny Mathis – Jakob Baekgaard 978-1-78952-247-1
Nu Metal: A Definitive Guide – Matt Karpe 978-1-78952-063-7
Tommy Bolin: In and Out of Deep Purple – Laura Shenton 978-1-78952-070-5
Maximum Darkness – Deke Leonard 978-1-78952-048-4
The Twang Dynasty – Deke Leonard 978-1-78952-049-1

and many more to come!

Would you like to write for Sonicbond Publishing?

At Sonicbond Publishing we are always on the look-out for authors, particularly for our two main series:

On Track. Mixing fact with in depth analysis, the On Track series examines the work of a particular musical artist or group. All genres are considered from easy listening and jazz to 60s soul to 90s pop, via rock and metal.

On Screen. This series looks at the world of film and television. Subjects considered include directors, actors and writers, as well as entire television and film series. As with the On Track series, we balance fact with analysis.

While professional writing experience would, of course, be an advantage the most important qualification is to have real enthusiasm and knowledge of your subject. First-time authors are welcomed, but the ability to write well in English is essential.

Sonicbond Publishing has distribution throughout Europe and North America, and all books are also published in E-book form. Authors will be paid a royalty based on sales of their book.

Further details are available from www.sonicbondpublishing. co.uk. To contact us, complete the contact form there or email info@sonicbondpublishing.co.uk